THE ULTIMATE VIDEO GAME TRIVIA BOOK

A Collection of Interesting Video Game History and Fun Facts for Gamers of All Ages

Jimmy Olsen

ISBN: 979-8-89095-036-9

TABLE OF CONTENTS

ATTENTION:

DO YOU WANT MY FUTURE BOOKS AT HEAVY DISCOUNTS AND EVEN FOR FREE?

HEAD OVER TO WWW.SECRETREADS.COM AND JOIN MY SECRET BOOK CLUB!

INTRODUCTION

No matter what your age is (unless you're over 75), you'll know that video games have been an important part of our culture for decades. Most people lucky enough to have grown up in areas with the technology will have memories of video games from early arcade classics to immersive cinematic experiences. Video games are a unique form of entertainment, creating unique bonds and memories that are harder-hitting than songs and longer-lasting than movies. This book will take you on a thrilling trek through gaming history as we explore classic titles, unforgettable characters, and the hidden stories that made us fall in love with gaming.

Each chapter will focus on a category of video games. You will probably have already scoured through the Table of Contents to find out what chapters to look at! Don't skip the introduction though, this is very important. The chapters will provide you with a multitude of information about games within the category. This could include innovations in gameplay, bizarre storylines, game-breaking bugs, hidden Easter eggs, and stories about the industry that is developing at a faster rate than any other in the world.

This book will examine legendary, un-ignorable titles such as *Pac-Man* and *Sonic the Hedgehog* while taking a glance at games that may have passed some of our younger readers by such as *Metal Gear Solid* or *DRIVER*. You'll discover the secret of *Pac-Man*'s origin, *Alien: Isolation*'s groundbreaking AI, and how *Left 4 Dead 2* managed to transform the co-op gaming genre.

Get ready to fall in love with the gaming greats all over again! Experience counts when it comes to gaming, but if you're not yet familiar with it all, don't worry! Whether you're an experienced gamer or aspire to become one, this book will help you find your next fantasy, or if you're unlucky, your next obsession.

Enjoy your journey through the annuls of the history of gaming. As you read, have YouTube open on a tablet or computer. Seriously, you'll want to quickly search up the game's footage so you can see what's been written about the game itself.

CHAPTER I: THE CLASSICS

This first chapter focuses, quite rightly, on some of the *classics*. These are some of the long-lasting giants of the video game industry. You'll hear about the stories behind the stories and the origins of the most famous games of all time.

1. MARIO: FROM PLUMBER TO MOVIE STAR IN 30 SHORT YEARS

Donning his blue overalls, red cap, and Pringles man-esque mustache, Mario is probably the most famous video game character *ever*. The Italian plumber first appeared in 1981, in *Donkey Kong*. He was originally named "Jumpman." He was renamed in later games, perhaps because the creator Shigeru Miyamoto foresaw that there'd be other video game characters who had the ability to jump, so Jumpman was a bad choice.

The rumor goes that the character was re-named Mario after the landlord of Nintendo's office in Seattle, Mario Segale. Mario's distinctive look was born almost entirely out of practicality. He wears a cap because the hair was especially difficult to animate in the 1980s, and the mustache was to emphasize his nose due to limited pixel resolution. Mario would later learn to live without his cap in later games, such as *Super Mario Odyssey*, perhaps to simply prove that after all this time he wasn't bald as many people had assumed.

Since his creation in the early 1980s, Mario, the cheerful Italian plumber who has saved the Mushroom Kingdom countless times, has become a universally recognized symbol of video games. As mentioned, Mario first appeared as Jumpman in 1981 and worked as a carpenter instead of a plumber. We've attempted to reach out to Mario about his career change, but he's been reluctant to respond thus far.

Once he shirked the name of a sub-par Marvel superhero, Mario was given his signature job as a plumber in 1983's *Mario Bros*, to fit the game's underground setting. This game also introduced Luigi, Mario's younger and taller brother. The brothers' Italian heritage was a nod to their profession; in the 1980s, pop culture often stereotyped plumbers as being Italian.

Mario remained a silent protagonist until 1995 when Charles Martinet was chosen to provide his voice. Martinet almost missed his audition but managed to arrive just as the casting director was leaving. He imagined Mario as a warm and friendly character and improvised a high-pitched Italian accent that was a stark contrast to the gruff Brooklyn accent Nintendo had originally requested. This voice, full of charm and whimsy, perfectly encapsulated Mario's spirit and has been his standard ever since. The gaming world, and Nintendo especially, owes a lot to Martinet for recognizing that the Brooklyn accent wouldn't have suited Mario. Martinet would go on to voice Mario for decades and can even be heard as a cameo in the 2023 *Mario Movie*.

Mario's design is filled with hidden nods to real-world influences. His love for pasta and pizza in various games is a playful tribute to his Italian heritage. His power-up transformations, such as the

Fire Flower that allows him to throw fireballs, were inspired by folklore and mythology. Even the game's settings, such as the Mushroom Kingdom, have roots in real-world locations; Miyamoto has stated that the game's world was inspired by his experiences exploring the countryside around his home in Kyoto, Japan as a child.

Mario was originally supposed to ride a dinosaur in the first *Super Mario Bros.* game, but technical limitations prevented this. The idea eventually resurfaced in *Super Mario World* with Yoshi, Mario's faithful dinosaur companion. Yoshi became a more permanent feature of the Mario universe from this point and is a fan favorite to this day.

Since that fortuitous appearance in the original *Donkey Kong* game, Mario has appeared in over 200 games, making him the most prolific video game character of all time. Through creative problem-solving, an innovative approach to character design, and a little bit of luck, Nintendo turned a simple 8-bit character into an enduring symbol of video games.

The Mario games transformed gaming and their impact can be seen in many games today. From the need for a recognizable, loveable protagonist to ensuring that puzzle platforming is well-considered and reasonably challenged, the influence is clear. Even if you're not an avid Nintendo gamer, you should take your cap off for Mario. Just don't ask him to do it or he might accidentally take on the power of a frog.

2. TETRIS: HELPING TO CURE PTSD

When you read the word "Tetris," it's very likely that you instantly picture the classic arcade game, in all its simple glory. *Tetris* is a game with a simple premise, simple controls, and a simple objective. The player must organize blocks, which slowly fall from the top of the screen to the bottom, in full lines. When that has happened, the blocks in the line disappear and the player gets points. The game isn't complicated but still draws millions of players every year, who play the latest iteration of the arcade staple.

Post-Traumatic Stress Disorder (PTSD) is a debilitating mental health disorder that affects people who have been through traumatic events such as war, disasters, accidents, or attacks. PTSD sufferers can experience a range of symptoms such as nightmares, panic attacks, flashbacks, and hallucinations. Researchers have looked for new ways to stop and treat PTSD over the years, and an unexpected hero has shown up in *Tetris*.

In an interesting study that was released in the journal *PLOS One*, researchers found that playing *Tetris* after a traumatic event may make it less likely that a person will develop PTSD. This finding shows how video games can have positive effects in the real world and offers a new way to study the link between gaming and mental health.

Video games require a set of skills, and *Tetris* is no exception. *Tetris* involves a lot of visual and spatial thinking, and players are encouraged to spin, move, and place shapes quickly. The "*Tetris* effect," which gets its name from the game, is when people keep seeing falling shapes and patterns even after they stop playing!

The PLOS One study looked at how *Tetris* might be able to stop visual memories, which are a sign of PTSD. Researchers thought that by using the same brain processes as playing *Tetris,* the game might stop traumatic memories from sticking and make it less likely that someone will get PTSD.

The study participants watched a film about a terrible event that was meant to make them feel bad. Then, half of the people played *Tetris* for 20 minutes, while the other half did something else. The data showed that the people who played *Tetris* had a lot fewer flashbacks than the people in the control group. The researchers thought that the fact that *Tetris* involves intensely focusing your eyes, might have disrupted the storage of painful memories, making it harder for flashbacks to happen.

There's a lot more to treating or preventing PTSD than playing *Tetris,* of course. Yet the study has opened up interesting questions about how we might go on to provide more effective treatment. More research still needs to be done to confirm these results, but the study suggests that playing *Tetris* right after a stressful event could be a simple, easy-to-do, and non-intrusive way to lower the risk of getting PTSD.

The study on PTSD and *Tetris* shows how video games can have effects outside of just being fun. Video games are a unique way to engage the mind and change behavior. They can help with everything from hand-eye coordination to fixing problems. Scientists are studying video games more and more to find out what benefits they might have in areas like improving brain function, mental health, therapy, and education.

3. PAC-MAN: LEFTOVER LUNCH TURNED HERO

Who's your favorite circular, yellow, ghost-chasing, dot-munching, 8-bit video game protagonist? Oh, Pac-Man? That's good - because that's what this chapter is about!

Pac-Man is a classic arcade game where you play as a yellow 2D circle that constantly makes a munching motion with its jaw. The circle navigates mazes, eating small dots; once all dots are eaten, the level is beaten (what a great rhyme). Ghosts roam around that take off a life if touched, however, and the game becomes incrementally more difficult to play the longer you play it.

The beloved character we all know boasts a simple yet distinct design that's hard to forget. Created by Toru Iwatani, this iconic video game has earned its place in history with its addictive gameplay and the character's unique appearance. The story of Pac-Man is shrouded in mystique, due to disparate stories around the character's origin.

Supposedly, Pac-Man's shape was inspired by Iwatanis's uneaten pizza with a single slice missing. Pac-Man's form is also said to be a simplified interpretation of "kuchi," which is Japanese for "mouth." As eating is Pac-Man's primary activity in gameplay, it makes perfect sense. In Japan, Pac-Man was initially introduced as "Puck Man" due to its similar resemblance to a hockey puck. However, the developers earned their award for "best prediction of a video game audience's childishness" when they realized that "Puck Man" can easily be graffitied to say something far ruder. Thus, Puck Man was changed to Pac-Man.

Notably different from other popular games of its time *like Space Invaders,* Iwatani developed Pac-Man with gender inclusivity in mind so both men and women could enjoy it equally. The game, being based on the universal human experience of eating and situated in a maze-like environment, was relatable for people from all walks of life.

Pac-Man also proved to be an intensely addictive experience for gamers. The accessibility of the first levels mixed with the tiny margins that can end a successful run had gamers hooked. The introduction of "power-ups" in Pac-Man marked a historic milestone for video games. The larger dots called "energizers" enabled players to consume the ghosts while maneuvering through the mazes. The revolutionary feature elevated this game's strategic gameplay experience above all others at the time.

In its simplicity lay one of *Pac-Man*'s major strengths: it appealed broadly without sacrificing uniqueness. This made *Pac-Man* an instant classic among gamers who could relate to his unending hunger in pursuit of overcoming identifiable barriers, in this case, the never-ending ghosts hunting him down! *Pac-Man* is re-produced and re-released every year in new and exciting ways and continues to boast competitions to challenge decades-old records.

4. SONIC THE HEDGEHOG: THE SPRINT FOR SUCCESS

Sonic the Hedgehog marks an interesting landmark in video game history. *Sonic* was created by SEGA to help them break into the console market, which was controlled by Nintendo. *Sonic*'s seemingly never-ending appeal enabled SEGA to gain a foothold in the market. The company then went on to develop a remarkable run of famous, notable, groundbreaking games. But it wouldn't have had that platform without *Sonic*'s success.

The character of Sonic's origin wasn't entirely organic. SEGA held a contest to come up with a figure that could be as popular as Nintendo's Mario, which Sonic won. SEGA wanted Sonic to represent the company in every aspect of his design. Sonic's blue color matches SEGA's logo, as well as helpfully representing a stylistic opposite to Mario's design. Sonic was adorned with bright red boots, markedly similar to those made famous by Michael Jackson, and this only helped his character design appeal more to kids, who flocked to buy the new games.

Yuji Naka, the co-creator of *Sonic the Hedgehog* series, loved pinball mechanics, which led to Sonic being able to roll up into a ball and attack foes. His speed, which is a key part of his character, was added so that the SEGA Genesis system could use all of its processing power.

Sonic's key characteristic and a staple of his gameplay is his speed. The designers liked the mechanics and physics of playing pinball, so attempted to employ this in the *Sonic* games. Sonic rolls up like a ball, enabling him to attack enemies, and achieves blisteringly fast speeds that leave some gamers unable to keep up. Sonic's lightning-fast sprinting showed gamers what the SEGA Genesis system was capable of, a feat that other competitors weren't yet able to replicate.

Sonic was made to have an attitude that SEGA thought would appeal to people growing up in the 1990s. He was sly and disrespectful, and he was the perfect example of the unruly spirit that SEGA wanted to show in their challenge to Nintendo and Mario, which conveyed a far more family-friendly style. In fact, SEGA took it a bit too far with Sonic's initial design. At first, he was supposed to be a band member with a real girlfriend named Madonna. But these ideas were thrown out because they made the figure too complicated.

Sonic was, in many ways, a gamble for SEGA. They pinned a lot on his success, and it paid off in the long term. Since the 1990s, there's been a cooling in competition between SEGA and Nintendo, which has led to Mario and Sonic being playable in the same game on multiple occasions. Notably, in *Super Smash Bros.*, the two characters can fight each other, reliving the heady days of the 90s. Sonic remains a turning point for SEGA, and the company (and gaming) is still shaped by the character.

5. DONKEY KONG: POPEYE'S LOSS IS THE WORLD'S GAIN

Donkey Kong's story as a character is so interesting, having changed more than almost any other video game figure. Donkey Kong started out as a villain, but later he became one of Nintendo's most popular heroes. We've already touched upon his first outing in the *Mario* section above. He graced screens in 1981 after his design by Shigeru Miyamoto and was, of course, the titular character in *Donkey Kong*. The "Donkey" part of this name was to signify stubbornness, while "Kong" was a popular way to refer to a gorilla in Japan at the time.

In *Donkey Kong*, the ape took Pauline hostage, and the player had to save her by playing Jumpman, who we know later became Mario. Donkey Kong would throw barrels at Jumpman in a series of challenging platforming levels. Initially, the game was designed to be a Popeye game, with Kong as Bluto, Mario as Popeye, and Pauline as Olive Oyl. The licensing was difficult to secure, however, so Miyamoto designed original characters.

When *Donkey Kong Country* came out for the Super Nintendo, *Donkey Kong* became a lot more well-known. In this game, Donkey Kong shifted from being the bad guy to being the main character. The whole game was about his adventures. The character's style also changed over time, dropping his sharp teeth and bellows, which gave him a friendlier vibe that made him a player favorite.

Donkey Kong is also one of the few video game characters who has ever been in a legal fight. In 1982, Universal Studios tried to sue Nintendo, saying that Donkey Kong stole their idea for King Kong. But they lost the case because it was shown that the story of King Kong and the figures in it were in the public domain. Thank goodness that giant apes had been an idea for so long, or Donkey Kong might have stayed in 1981, an angry ape on a forgotten arcade machine.

Donkey Kong remains a firm favorite across the world, and gamers look back fondly at the characters that have developed from the early days of one giant, frustrated, ape. Nintendo faces constant calls on social media for new *Donkey Kong* games, which have achieved constant critical and commercial success.

DID YOU KNOW: EASTER EGGS

If you're one of those gamers who spend their time seeking out every secret in the game, trying out specific circumstances, testing bizarre commands, and maybe even going so far as accessing the game files to unearth the mysteries, well, after this chapter you need to say out loud (unless you're on a train):

"Thanks, Warren Robinett, for ruining my social life! You're the best!"

In 1979, Warren Robinett had been finishing up his work on the game *Adventure,* a title by Atari. Atari had rules back then about taking credit for a game's development. Developers worked in a team and that team was the Atari team, so that's who got the collective credit, not the individual. Warren thought, "Well, that won't do" and decided to do something that changed video game development forever, all in the name of getting his name seen by spotty teenagers staring at a computer roughly the size of the Millennium Falcon.

He decided to create a secret within the game that would show his credit. It's since been termed an "Easter egg." If you're not someone who celebrates Easter, Easter eggs are traditionally hidden on Easter Sunday and then kids go and hunt them down. This is precisely what the idea was for Robinett's credit.

Robinett hid an on-pixel object called "Gray Dot," which blended into its surroundings behind an object named "The Key." Finding the object would give players access to a room where Robinett's creator credit was situated. Players found this bizarre secret and set about trying to find it in other games as well. Pretty soon, every developer was putting some sort of difficult-to-discover secret in their games, giving gamers an extra mission to attempt while playing.

Robinett's creative Easter egg idea is now firmly rooted in the history of video games. This secret creator credit was a significant milestone that took gaming behavior to a whole new level. Easter eggs are now the topic of literally millions of videos and discussion boards across the internet. Some are small references to pop culture or simply a new weapon. But the most celebrated ones are those that are elaborate in the set-up and the execution or may even change the gaming experience as a whole.

Much like hunting for treasure, this became an immersive experience that caught on worldwide! Even today countless undiscovered gems are waiting patiently for discovery within various video game titles - all unique and each with their own story but all of which started with *Adventure*'s Easter egg! Warren Robinett's courageous move when creating *Adventure* helped pave the way for future developers who sought new ways of designing exciting gameplay while inspiring fans everywhere with innovative ideas.

Here are seven quick Easter eggs for you to hunt out while on your gaming travels!

1. If you play through *Silent Hill 2,* unlocking three "normal" endings, then you unlock the secret dog ending. This ending tells you that the nightmarish events that unfolded in the horror game were all controlled by a Shiba Inu, a little cute dog. It's fun but takes a serious grind to get to!
2. If you play *Hitman 3,* then pay close attention to the secret exit at the Berlin level. Earlier in the level, you'll find some UFO graffiti. Take a picture of it, complete the level as normal, then run to the telephone booth by the gas station and dial "1993." You won't leave via the front door, but instead by a gigantic alien spaceship.
3. *Naughty Dog* hid some fantastic hints alluding to their other projects in their games. In 2011's *Uncharted 3,* a newspaper can be spotted with the headline: "Scientists still struggling to understand deadly fungus." This is a very clear reference to the legendary game *Last of Us* which would be released two years later.
4. The *Grand Theft Auto* series is well known for its sense of humor and little pop culture references. In *Grand Theft Auto V,* you can find an obvious, in-your-face reference to the 1991 hit *Thelma & Louise.* The movie famously ends with the two female protagonists cornered by police in a convertible on the edge of a cliff. Together, they hold hands and drive off of the cliff in a blaze of glory. Well, if you fly a helicopter by Raton Canyon between 7 and 8 p.m., you'll find a perfect recreation of this famous and beloved shot.

5. The *Borderlands* games love a little nod to the broader gaming community and in *Borderlands 2*, they make a fantastic and surprising reference to *Minecraft*. In the Caustic Caverns, some dirt cubes are to be found. After striking them, a series of creeper enemies straight from Minecraft come rushing out to the player. There's some great Minecraft-inspired loot too, but it's that big shock the creeper provides that makes it most fun for the player.
6. If you're a bit of a *Marvel* buff, then you probably get a kick out of the later *Spider-Man* games. When you've got some time on your hands, web yourself around NYC and tick off locations from the Marvel Cinematic Universe. There are plenty to find from the Avenger's Tower to Tony Stark's Department of Damage Control.
7. In *Metal Gear Solid 3*, players eventually face off against *The End*, a deadly sniper. The level can take a lot of time and be very frustrating. If you're quick and accurate, however, you can take him out early when he's first spotted at *Ponizovje Warehouse*. Or you can set your PlayStation's date forward by a week, and he'll die of old age.

CHAPTER II:
ACTION/ADVENTURE

Leaving behind some of the early heroes of video gaming, this chapter will now examine the broad genre of Action/Adventure. It's a strange one. What does it actually mean? Most video games have *some* form of adventure within them unless it's basically a board game like Mahjong or an "I'm bored game" like FIFA. Action/Adventure games, however, typically involve a lot of sequences that are thrilling and dangerous and a storyline that leads you through exciting, ever-changing scenes to unravel the full game. Many games have elements of Action/Adventure in them, but here is a small selection of some notable and incredible examples of this far-reaching genre.

6. LARA CROFT: HOW THE TOMB RAIDER CAME TO BE

The creation of Lara Croft, the iconic *Tomb Raider,* an archaeologist and warrior, notorious for her bravery in the action game series, traces back to 1996.

Toby Gard was engaged by Core Design, a British game company, to create Lara Croft. The artist wanted to revolutionize action-adventure games dominated by male characters at that time. Gard drew on significant influence from cultural icons of the late 20th century. *Indiana Jones* was an ideal model for his adventures in excavation while *Tank Girls'* tough and independent nature appealed equally.

Lara Croft was initially designed to be a muscular man inspired by the *Prince of Persia* game character. The decision to create Lara as a female character was made mainly because of the intense competition in the genre at the time. Almost all action-adventure characters (in fact, almost all video game characters in general) in the 90s were male. Credit is due to Gard for seeing that creating yet another one would do little for the video game market..., and little for their sales.

The initial design of the iconic character was a South American woman named Laura Cruz but was later changed to Lara Croft. Croft's adventures are grand and undoubtedly expensive. She also possesses a broad range of skills and knowledge, so her back story had to explain these.

Lara was written to be an affluent British aristocrat who pursued adventure using the wealth she inherited from her family. Her affluent background rendered her ability to undertake these elaborate missions believable. Gard also took inspiration for Lara's character from pop culture icons of his time along with real-life influences. In the 80s and 90s, movies like *Jurassic Park* and *Indiana Jones* spurred interest in archaeology, which led to Lara being an archeologist.

Controversy emerged surrounding Lara Croft's appearance soon after her debut in the gaming world. The media brought attention to the fact that her chest was oversized or "too big" for an action hero that was supposed to be taken seriously. It turns out that this came about accidentally when there was a mistake with digital avatars' alterations during design. The error remained way through production when graphic designers mistakenly increased the chest size nearly twice its original dimensions. This programming glitch brought wide attention to the gaming series. The design of future *Tomb Raider* games has made sure that Lara Croft has a more representative figure that is more realistic in regard to her career as, well, a tomb-raider.

Interestingly, Lara holds two Guinness World Records: one for being the "Most Recognizable Female Video Game Character" and another for being the "Most Detailed Video Game Character." The *Tomb Raider* franchise has been so successful that it expanded beyond video games into books, animated shows, and two full-length films featuring Angelina Jolie and Alicia Vikander as Lara Croft.

Looking back at the creation of one of gaming's most famous characters, we can see the odd role that accident, chance, fate, or whatever you want to call it, played in Lara's inception. She's remained a staple of the action series and a character that players, particularly female ones, identify with, and for that she's irreplaceable.

7. UNCHARTED: CINEMA MEETS GAMING

The main criticism of action gaming is that it can be repetitive and occasionally dull. Action games haven't always pushed the envelope of ingenuity, instead opting for repetitive gameplay and the same old ways of gaming. It's the same criticism directed at action movies. At times, the genre is too constrictive to truly have fun with it.

This is where *Uncharted* comes in.

The first game in the series was introduced in 2007 for the PlayStation 3. The PS3 brought a fresh sense of excitement when it was released, promising to propel gaming forward with its exceptional hardware and capabilities. *Uncharted: Drake's Fortune* was supposed to allow Sony and Naughty Dog to show off just what the engine could do.

The game became an instant classic and sparked a franchise around the charismatic and witty adventurer Nathan Drake. He embarked on daring journeys in search of lost treasures, facing perilous challenges and ruthless enemies (as well as hordes of anonymous henchmen, but every action game needs those).

What truly set the game apart was its ingenuity and innovations within the genre of Action/Adventure. Naughty Dog sought to bring a sense of cinema to the series. The storytelling and seamless gameplay left players feeling like they were writing the script of their own Hollywood blockbuster. Naughty Dog had no problem allowing a natural conversation to take place, with humorous dialogue or even slightly banal topics for chatter. The games ebbed and flowed like an *Indiana Jones* film, much to Naughty Dog's credit.

It might be fair to say that action games had become slightly stale in the early 2000s. Platforming is an intrinsic part of the genre and needs constant innovation. Platforming is the action of moving around a dynamic level. This involves not simply traveling from A to B in a linear line but traveling from A up to D back to B before having to travel to Z to M and then finally landing at C, which you weren't expecting. *Uncharted* brought a fluid version of platforming to the mainstream video game industry, and many series followed suit after. The 2010s *Tomb Raider* titles and *Assassin's Creed* games are two obvious examples that benefited from *Uncharted.*

Uncharted was an immediate success. The series has sold over 41 million copies over its titles and Nathan Drake became a figurehead for PlayStation 3. All games in the series have received glowing reviews from critics around the world, and video games have benefited from the blueprint of storytelling left behind. *The Last of Us* and the *God of War* series took inspiration from *Uncharted*'s storytelling to become best sellers in the 2020s.

Uncharted is a testament to innovation and pushing the boundaries. The game could have slipped into the annuls of gaming history with little fanfare, the basic concept seemed so "meh." But the execution was nothing short of spectacular, and the games are well worth playing through today.

8. BIOSHOCK: BLURRING GENRES

"Hey boss, I have an idea for a game."

"Go on, I'm listening."

"We send the player into the depths of the ocean for an unknown reason, into a steampunk city where they encounter frightening rogue-AI enemies, huge, terrifying enemies called 'Big Daddy,' and they also have superpowers."

"Sounds great, let's do it."

This is how one imagines the conversation must have gone at Irrational Games when they conceptualized the *Bioshock* games.

The series was launched in 2007 with its titular game *Bioshock.* The game was a genuine sensation for gamers at the time, all because of *that* opening scene, as you enter the underwater city of Atlas, which hooked players in and wouldn't let them go until they'd finished the whole thing. Players felt like a delighted Bruce Bogtrotter in *Matilda* if Brucey had been forced to play through a genuine nightmare instead of eating a big cake.

Bioshock weaved together an experience full of horror and reflection on society that was unparalleled at the time. Horror games were in their own zone, with little touching them. Franchises such as *Resident Evil* and *Silent Hill* had horror down, and the genre bounced between new titles that raised their head before falling to the wayside.

(SPOILERS!) In *Bioshock,* the players are guided through Atlas by Andrew Ryan, someone who seemingly is on your side throughout your horrifying experience. The famous reveal at the end of the game brings the preconceptions that gamers hold crashing down as the player realizes the level of manipulation they've experienced. Through shrewd manipulation of interactive gameplay mechanics, BioShock highlighted for its users just how limited agency remains for any given character within games - shaking up some assumptions players may hold regarding their perceived independence throughout playtime.

Bioshock made players believe the game was a free-flowing journey, and they only discovered later that it was completely pre-determined throughout. All preceding decisions a player had made were essentially illusions managed to maintain the piece of storyline driving specifically for this important reveal at the climax.

Replaying BioShock in the light of this vital twist reveals the second significant impact: We thought BioShock was just a survival tale tied with political conspiracies but discovered a story instead filled with critical philosophical examinations of objectivism, power-related self-destruction, and moral quandaries raising tough ethical questions regarding autonomy versus controlling systems.

As a pioneer in immersive gaming experiences, *BioShock* blurred the genre lines more than many games had done before. The game transforms in front of the player as they play it, moving from horror to a storytelling game, to a superhero game, and finally to a piece of political commentary. *Bioshock* was incredibly innovative for the time and helped show the action genre that the rules aren't only to be bent - they can be broken, snapped, ground down, and remodeled to be whatever you want them to be.

9. TITANFALL 2: FALLING IN LOVE WITH A MASSIVE ROBOT

(MAJOR SPOILERS FOR *TITANFALL 2*)

Titanfall was released in 2014 and players took to it quickly. A quick summary of its gameplay is: You're in a massive robot and you fight each other in a futuristic combat style. It doesn't sound that amazing, does it?

Well, *Titanfall 1* wasn't really that incredible. It had no single-player mode, boasting an online mode only, but it was incredibly fun. The robots were agile, free-running creations, and were *huge.* Few games had as exhilarating combat, and the series offered something sillier and more casual than the other combat games such as *Call of Duty (CoD)* and *Battlefield.*

In 2016, *Titanfall* 2 was released by Respawn Entertainment and left a surprisingly big mark on the action genre.

The second game had to bring something new - there is only so far you can go with "big robot shoots things" - and the studio delivered. Many fans were excited to learn that there would be a single-player mode in *Titanfall 2,* while others were skeptical.

Games known for being online normally have a pretty dull single player, which serves to simply get the player to compete online. Again, *CoD* is a perfect example of a series that thrives online, and whose single player is essentially the "add-on." Sports games such as *FIFA, NBA,* and *Madden* are also notable for this phenomenon.

The single-player mode is short; gamers can complete it in eight hours comfortably, even less if they decide to be a bit more slapdash about it. You play as Jack Cooper, a new Titan (the big robot) pilot who is thrown into a war zone and forced to adapt and quickly advance well beyond his basic training. He takes over a Titan called BT-7274, and their bond forms almost instantly; and with this, the players' bond does too.

The campaign was nothing short of exhilarating. Constant gunfights, innovation in gameplay, time out of the Titan, time in the Titan, explosions, clever dialogue, and an unraveling story. Gamers were left genuinely gob-smacked that a title that was seen as a fun online game could boast such creativity in its single-player.

The movement mechanics have only improved from *Titanfall 1,* with the parkour system working as intuitively as *Mirrors Edge* and the synergy between man and machine never feeling clunky. The gameplay was dynamic and freeing, and the storyline was…, crushing.

(SPOILER!) By the end of *Titanfall 2,* you are well and truly best friends with a fictional robot. So well-crafted is the story that BT-7274 became an unexpected favorite in gaming communities around the world. This made his death even more devastating.

In one of the final missions, the Titan sacrifices himself for Jack, and the loss of a FAKE ROBOT left gamers heartbroken.

The game received critical acclaim for its daring single-player and the improved multiplayer experience. *Titanfall 2* has gone on to have somewhat of a cult following, with communities still playing the 2016 game online. For seven years, gamers have asked about the potential for *Titanfall 3,* but we are yet to see a sign that any such game is imminent. The franchise is a surprising example of innovation in mechanics and storytelling, and it is thoroughly deserving of the love it receives from its fans.

10. LEGEND OF ZELDA: KEEPING IT LEGENDARY AND INNOVATIVE

Yes, yes, obviously this game should be in *The Classics* section as well, but there are too many classics. It'll have to languish here in Chapter Two.

The first *Legend of Zelda* game came out in 1986 for the Nintendo Entertainment System (NES). It was made by a Japanese game creator named Shigeru Miyamoto. Miyamoto got the idea for the game from the time he spent as a child exploring the woods, caves, and lakes near his home. Yes, by the way, it's *that* Shigeru Miyamoto from *Mario* and *Donkey Kong*. The man is responsible for about 20% of the world's childhood gaming!

Action/Adventure games have changed a lot since the first Legend of Zelda game came out. It was the first game to have non-linear gameplay, a big open world, and a save function that let players keep going. Link is the main character in the series, his name coming from the idea that he is a "link" between the player and the world of the game. He is famous for his green tunic, hat, and sword, and for trying to save Princess Zelda and beat Ganon, the main bad guy.

As of 2021, more than 125 million versions of the *Legend of Zelda* games have been sold around the world. It has become one of Nintendo's most popular and long-lasting series, with a lot of sequels, spin-offs, and versions for different systems.

The series is known for its recurring elements, like the Triforce, a sacred object that gives its owner power, knowledge, and courage, and the Master Sword, a legendary weapon that Link often uses.

To define the *Legend of Zelda*'s impact is to define Action games in general. Zelda sets the standard for the mechanics of an action/adventure game and has done a fantastic job of reinventing them as the years have gone by. Think of how many games you have that require you to "loot," or find secret objects or collectibles. It's almost all of them. This role-playing element of upgrading weapons and statistics that *Legends of Zelda* pioneered is now a staple in most games - even *The SIMS* has that.

Many (older) gamers will posit that the best game of all time is *The Legend of Zelda: Ocarina of Time (OoT),* which came out for the Nintendo 64 in 1998. They'd have a good point. The *Zelda* series was already innovative, but *OoT* was the first game to have a 3D world, hard puzzles, and a way to move through time so that players could experience different parts of the story. In 1998, this was exceptionally impressive. Some systems then were still producing games that played more like a PowerPoint presentation than an exciting adventure!

In recent years, the series has redefined itself as a huge open-world game series with its Nintendo Switch games. This has caused genuine debate as to whether *these* are the best games of all time.

The series' examination of themes such as heroism, fate, and the balance of good and bad power makes for a thrilling playthrough. Gamers have stayed loyal to the franchise for good reasons. The care and precision put into each game in the franchise has kept it fresh even after nearly 40 years.

DID YOU KNOW: ASSASSIN'S CREED

Have you heard of *Assassin's Creed*? Of course, you have, you're a gamer reading this book, aren't you? The series is almost impossible to escape and if you managed that, there was a film with Michael Fassbender in it produced in the 2010s! Admittedly, it was terrible, but you get the point.

The Assassin's Creed games put you in a historical setting, playing as a free-running, silky-smooth assassin. You go through a variety of missions that build toward a dramatic finale, where your influence is felt in whatever era you are in. The game has visited Renaissance Italy, Ancient Egypt, and Victorian London, and has even let you be a buccaneering pirate in the 18th century.

The game is known for being a bit of a hit-and-miss when it comes to execution, with some titles being rather dull for such a thrilling concept while others are exhilarating. But over the last 15 years, the *Assassin's Creed* franchise has been a mainstay of the Action/Adventure genre. Here are a few facts about the games that you may not have been so aware of.

The series is known for being surprisingly historically accurate and paying close attention to detail when recreating famous places and times. As mentioned before, the games have taken place in many different times and places. This has required particularly impressive historical recreation, most noticeably in the wake of the 2019 fire at the famed cathedral in Paris, Notre Dame. Since then, work has been undertaken to attempt to restore the famous medieval building, and the Assassin's Creed team have been invaluable. In *Assassin's Creed Unity*, Notre Dame was depicted, which means they created an almost-perfect 3D model of the great cathedral. This model has been given over to help in the restoration process.

1. *Assassin's Creed* is, perhaps unsurprisingly, Ubisoft's best-selling franchise. In 2023, the total number of titles sold is somewhere around 200 million. Ubisoft aims for one title per year or two. In a pattern similar to blockbusters such as *Call of Duty*, the aim is to sell the game every December. This ensures the game is out for Christmas and on the list of over a half of the gamers in North America.

2. Arguably, the Disney movie *Frozen* wouldn't be the same without *Assassin's Creed*. Kristen Bell, the actor who played Anna in the global sensation, had her debut voice acting credit in the first *Assassin's Creed* way back in 2007. She continued to voice Lucy Stillman in the franchise and has gone on to become as much of a successful voice actor as she is a screen actor.

3. Originally, *Assassin's Creed* wasn't supposed to be *Assassin's Creed*. While in production, it was supposed to be a *Prince of Persia* game. The *Prince of Persia* games had been popular

during the early 2000s and Ubisoft was planning to bring it to PlayStation 3. The concept was that you'd play an assassin in the employ of the prince, but Ubisoft didn't like the idea. Rather than scrap the whole project, *Assassin's Creed* was conceptualized, the work was adapted, and here we are 15 years later.

4. You'd be forgiven for thinking that there is no end in sight to the *Assassin's Creed* series. Currently, they have released 12 main titles, with the latest being *Valhalla* in 2020. There have also been 16 spin-off titles released, and Ubisoft has planned for the next four games, which will be *Mirage, Codename Red, Codename Hexe,* and *Codename Jade*. There is also to be a multiplayer game soon after *Mirage* called *Project Invictus*. This will bring the franchise to more than 30 games! Ubisoft says they have a plan for its end and know when that will be, but they have no desire to impart that information just yet (nor part with the potential billions that it will bring in).

5. If you're more of a reader than a watcher (or noticed that the reviews for the movie were awful) then you may be interested in the novels surrounding *Assassin's Creed*. There are currently ten on offer, which is plenty to get stuck into even for an expert reader. It's good not to stare at a screen sometimes, you know.

6. Ezio Auditore, one of the series' more beloved assassins, has actually made the leap to another universe of games. In 2012, the fighting game *Soulcalibur V*, was released and Ezio was made a playable character. With some pithy dialogue and a fun set of moves, he became a fan favorite, though didn't return. After all, he had some Creeding to get back to.

CHAPTER III:
SCARE-TASTIC THRILLERS

Remain calm, try not to wet yourself, and for god's sake, ask permission from your parents before playing these games!

This chapter is all about the scary games that have been produced over the years. The horror genre has the capacity to recycle tired ideas, in both movies and video games. It's easy to shove a few jump scares in and make sure there's plenty of blood. These titles provided something more innovative or important for the horror genre. This chapter will tell you about five of the greatest games that have players checking under their beds for scary monsters, even years after they were released.

11. ALIEN ISOLATION: THE MOST TERRIFYING AI EVER DEVISED

If you ask someone to tell you what the best dystopian-sci-fi-horror franchise of the 1980s is, then they should say *Alien*. If they don't, and instead say *Predator*, then politely remind them that most of the *Predator* movies are garbage.

Alien has remained a constant and prominent feature of the horror landscape since it first graced the big screen in 1980. The terrifying two mouths of the xenomorph, with no visible eyes, endless drool and domineering figure, make it one heck of a specimen. If you're of the right age, go and watch *Alien*; even though it's an old movie, it holds up surprisingly well as one of the greats.

Of course, along with this movie franchise have come video games set in the universe of *Alien*. It makes sense - it's an already established character with a fantastic full world created around it, so why not make games about Alien? The problem is that the *Alien* games have been a mixed bag at best. Some, such as *Alien vs. Predator*, were fun but oddly disorientating (you may vomit from motion sickness playing this) while some, like *Alien: Colonial Marines,* were boring and bland.

This is where 2013's *Alien Isolation* comes in.

The game puts you in the 'first-person' perspective of Ellen Ripley's daughter, journeying to a large space station. At one time a vibrant hub of shopping and leisure, when you arrive you find the space station to be in disrepair and eerily quiet. After some exploring and a *very* tense atmosphere, you first lay eyes on the xenomorph that has reduced this floating metropolis to a disaster zone.

For the rest of the game, your job is to evade the Alien, whose entire mission is to hunt *you* down and kill you. You cannot kill the xenomorph (well, you can, but you're not supposed to be able to) and you cannot outrun it - you can only hide from it.

The game is sickeningly scary. The xenomorph is in constant "find" mode and is extremely sensitive to sound. So, if you rush a movement, or knock over something in your travels, it will make a beeline to your location and hunt you down.

The idea was sound from the get-go, but the big question was "How can this game be made fair?"

This was accomplished through an ingenious "double-AI." In the open world of the ship, the Alien is controlled by its own AI. Alien AI actively listens and searches for the player, seeking cues to help locate them. This can be difficult, and a good player could get through the game making no noise, which is where the second AI comes in.

The second AI acts as a director. It gives hints to the Alien, telling it to investigate an area if it's been a while without much conflict. This gives the constant feeling of "the Alien is never far away." The director AI also tells the Alien to leave if it's been in one location too long, or if the player has hidden for a long time. This is to keep up the pace and to keep the game somewhat fair for the player.

The result is a seamless horror experience that gives a truly unique experience to the player. The xenomorph doesn't just *feel* like it's hunting you, it *is*. It's doing everything it can to get to you and there's little you can do about it!

Let's just say that players of *Alien Isolation* quickly become accustomed to dying....

12. SILENT HILL 2: JAMES SUNDERLAND'S TRUE ACTIONS

Silent Hill is one of those staple horror franchises. Other than *Resident Evil,* there's no more dominant force in the genre. Arguably, the series peaked in 2001 with *Silent Hill 2,* which took gaming horror to new depths.

Players were instantly drawn in by *Silent Hill 2.* Its spooky atmosphere, deep story, and psychological topics were new areas of interest for developers. The players take control of James Sunderland, a troubled man who gets a letter from his dead wife telling him to go back to the strange town of Silent Hill. James returns to the town, thinking that his wife Mary has somehow come back from the dead. On his journey, he meets strange people and fights freakish, body-horror-style creatures. The player fights to stay alive and discover the truth.

(BIG SPOILERS AHEAD!)

As players get deeper into the psychological horror of the game, creepy details start to come to light. Under the surface, a darker truth is hinted at with clues and symbols. James' real nature and actions start to become clear when he meets people like Angela, Eddie, and Maria, and a puzzle is slowly pieced together. In the game's climax, the players finally find the shocking truth out for themselves: James suffocated his dying wife Mary because he felt guilty and hopeless. He did this instead of letting her die normally from her illness.

The effects of this discovery are huge. It changes how the player perceives the game and James' character and actions throughout the game. James's search for his dead wife, which at first seemed like an act of love and devotion, turns out to be a journey of self-punishment and release. The story gets a new layer of psychological depth as it considers blame, loss, and how fragile human sanity is.

The town of Silent Hill becomes a physical representation of James's troubled mind. It forces him to face his inner demons and the effects of his actions. The game explores complex topics like fear, denial, and the ways people use their minds to protect themselves when they are ravaged by guilt.

The twist in *Silent Hill 2* forces players to question what they think they know and invites them to investigate the darker recesses of their own minds. The discovery shows how powerful video games can be in telling psychological and introspective stories, pushing the limits of what can be done in interactive stories.

The franchise went on to create many more horror classics, but it was *Silent Hill 2* that made the biggest impact. In the 2010s and 2020s, many horror games have taken the psychological angle to warp players' perceptions of events and to hide the full nature of what's going on. The *Amnesia* series is a notable example of *Silent Hill 2*'s influence.

13. DOOM II: THE JOHN ROMERO EASTER EGG

To play *Doom* is to become the boss fight, and that is an experience every gamer should have. The basic premise behind the *Doom* games is that demons have come into this reality and now need to be vanquished. That's basically that. You play as the 'Doomslayer', an almost-mute badass who masters a veritable arsenal of bone-crushing, meat-mincing, eyeball-popping weaponry to fight back the hordes from hell.

And it's very, very satisfying to always be the most powerful one in the room.

Doom has been around since the early 1990s and has always flirted with controversy for its excessive violence and gore. Of course, the gore of the 2020s is a *tad* more detailed than the 1990s, but it has always been a shocking game. It holds influence in the horror genre, not being afraid to push the boundaries of what gamer's stomachs can handle, but it has made other impacts as well.

Doom II, developed in 1994 by id Software, holds a particularly special place in gaming history. Within its intense and action-packed gameplay lies a hidden Easter egg that pays tribute to one of the game's key creators. In the final level of *Doom II,* players who manage to bypass a certain wall will come face to face with an unexpected sight - the head of game designer John Romero impaled on a pike!

The Easter egg was slyly installed into the game as a testament to the collaborative and spirited nature of id Software's development team. The Easter egg's existence remained a secret until players stumbled upon it, adding an element of surprise and delight to their gaming experience. This unexpected encounter immortalized Romero within the game, solidifying his status as a gaming legend and leaving an indelible mark on *Doom II*'s legacy.

Doom has never been afraid to have a bit of fun, even in the face of waves of hellish monsters, and this was a great example of it. One could write a book about *Doom,* its various iterations, and its cult stories. For example, Doom was banned in Germany until well into the 2010s! Also, the 2016 *Doom* soundtrack may very well be the most bracing soundtrack to a game of all time. Put it on next time you're doing exercise and try not to imagine yourself smashing and tearing demons apart in a pool of lava.

14. RESIDENT EVIL: CLAUSTROPHOBIC HORROR

In the dark and eerie world of survival horror, one series emerged as a definitive pioneer: *Resident Evil*. Developed by Capcom, the first installment of the series, simply went on to shape the horror genre and establish itself as a monumental titled *Resident Evil,* which debuted on March 22, 1996, on the PlayStation.

The *Resident Evil* series plunges players into terrifying situations, pitting them against hordes of zombies, grotesque creatures, and sinister conspiracies. The games follow different protagonists, often members of the elite Special Tactics and Rescue Service (S.T.A.R.S.) or other groups, as they navigate haunted mansions, abandoned facilities, and other nightmarish environments.

That first 1996 game is widely credited with popularizing the survival horror genre. It blended atmospheric storytelling, limited resources, and challenging puzzles with tense combat, delivering a heart-pounding and immersive experience. You don't have to look far to see how far the influence of survival horror has reached. From huge-budget blockbusters like *Last of*

Us, to smaller indie titles like *The Forest* and *Don't Starve,* most horror games are now survival horror to one degree or another.

The early *Resident Evil* games introduced the concept of "tank controls," which meant that players maneuvered their characters as if they were driving a tank. This system of control was clunky and not as intuitive as that of many other video games, which is perfect for a tense horror game. As the impending zombies walk toward the protagonist, the controls partially impede your ability to run away from or fight the danger. In later titles, Capcom abandoned this, but the series continued forcing players to feel as though they weren't fully in control of their circumstances.

Capcom's creative team also displayed impressive inventiveness from the first *Resident Evil* title. The creatures encountered are varied and often grotesque in nature. More recent titles such as *Village* or *Biohazard* play into the tropes of body horror, popularized in the 1980s by movies like *The Thing*. The bizarreness of the terror added to *Resident Evil*'s uniqueness, and its influence can be seen in countless modern horror games such as *The Evil Within.* This inventiveness has led *Resident Evil* to be adapted into a movie series, with its own cult following.

The most unique aspect of *Resident Evil,* however, remains its ability to create a sense of claustrophobia. Claustrophobia refers to fear generated from being cooped up or trapped in a small area. Capcom masterfully engineered this in 1996 and has continued to do so since. In *Resident Evil,* you're in a haunted mansion and forced to explore all manner of tiny rooms and thin corridors, while confronted with the terrifying creatures. In the more recent *Resident Evil: Biohazard,* you explore a small house while being chased by a psychotic family, intent on exacting a violent death upon you.

The game's ability to engineer a genuine fear that you are trapped is unique, and no horror series has come close to creating the sense of paranoia and "I have to get out of here" that *Resident Evil* manages. The game taps into your primal "fight or flight" response and forces you to confront the horror rather than run from it. *Resident Evil* is not a game full of cheap, easy frights; it's a game that pokes at your deeper, animalistic fears, and it does so expertly.

The horror landscape is promising in the 2020s, and it's because of games like *Resident Evil* that paved the way, constantly innovating and improving on the old styles and techniques.

15. DEAD SPACE: A STUDY INTO HOW QUICKLY A GAMER WILL UNINSTALL

If you're a younger gamer, younger than your early 20s, then you won't quite understand the effect that *Dead Space* had on gamers in 2008.

When EA Redwood Shores (later known as Visceral Games) released *Dead Space*, it became clear that something special had happened. By the late 2000s, the behemoths that were *Resident Evil* and *Silent Hill* were dropping off the radar, and production slowed on big-budget horror games. Online multiplayer was taking off with alarming speed, and the attention was on war games like *Call of Duty*. *Dead Space* set a new standard in horror gaming in 2008, and left gamers mesmerized and terrified at the world that had been developed.

The series follows the escapades of Isaac Clarke, an engineer in space. Clarke faces off against the nightmarish necromorphs, mutated corpses reanimated by an alien artifact known as the Marker. Armed with improvised weapons and his own intelligence, Clarke battles through claustrophobic corridors and isolated spacecraft, uncovering a conspiracy at every turn.

The game certainly drew on the elements of *Resident Evil* and *Silent Hill that* worked well. It created an air of genuine paranoia and tension about what might come around the corner to vicariate your character. *Dead Space* innovated in more technical ways that used the new power of the XBOX 360 and PlayStation 3, to flesh out a world that would have been impossible before.

In *Dead Space,* you can take apart the necromorphs through *strategic dismemberment.* This means that players could shoot at parts of the vile creatures to incapacitate them. Given the necromorphs' strength, this added a sense of tactics and strategy when fighting. It helped add depth to shooting and meant that players had to think before simply shooting at the bad guys.

Dead Space was also notable for its extremely innovative HUD. The HUD is the Heads-Up Display, which displays information vital for the player. HUDs have been in games forever; they display health, ammunition, objectives, collectables, you name it. However, the HUD can be distracting when trying to immerse gamers in their experience. How can they believe that they're destroying a space mutant if there's a big sign above their character's head saying "60% HEALTH, 20% ARMOR"? In *Dead Space,* the developers integrated all of the information that a HUD displays as part of Isaac's suit. The HUD data was now part of the scene, rather than projected over it, taking a revolutionary leap in offering a more encapsulating experience.

Dead Space was well received critically, and players from across the globe were in awe of the new leaps taken in 2008 to bring true horror to gamers. The first game has recently been remastered for the current generation of consoles, a testament to the everlasting terror of the series even 15 years after its creation.

DID YOU KNOW: ZOMBIES IN VIDEO GAMES

If we're talking about the Horror genre, we must talk about zombies. Zombies have been reliable antagonists in gaming for decades. Most people know what they are - reanimated dead people - and have no problem fighting them in-game. You can either make them slow, a looming threat, or you can allow them to run straight at the player, causing an instant panicked reaction.

This list is a quick rundown of some of the most notable zombie experiences from gaming history, in no particular order (excluding *Resident Evil* and *Dead Space*, which we've already covered, and *Last of Us*, which comes later). This list has been chosen based on the innovation or uniqueness in the design or execution of a zombie game. There are literally hundreds more that have taken inspiration from this list.

1. Left 4 Dead

Left 4 Dead was released by Valve Corporation in November 2008. *L4D*, as it was initiated, quickly became one of the most popular games around, drawing in millions on PC and XBOX. *L4D* is a co-operative game, meaning you have to work together (talking to you here, *Fortnite* players). Together, you play through levels that involve running away from hordes of zombies, some with special powers, to reach a difficult objective.

There's an overarching plot, the characters are funny, and the game is endlessly fun. By 2009, ten million copies had been sold, a feat that was bested by *Left 4 Dead 2* a couple of years later. *Left 4 Dead*'s zombie design was interesting enough to provide some variety, and the levels were varied and interesting, avoiding the "copy & paste" levels that some companies relied on.

The game made use of the "AI Director" that dynamically altered the gameplay to ensure that gamers could replay almost endlessly. *Left 4 Dead* was a phenomenon, and the gaming world has waited with bated breath for *L4D3* for a decade now, with no sign that it's on its way. *Back 4 Blood* was released in the 2020s and is about as close as they'll get for now.

2. Dying Light

Dying Light was released in 2015 by Techland which devised a unique angle for their zombie apocalypse.

In *Dying Light,* you navigate the complicated, dilapidated city with smooth, controllable parkour. The game was expert at lulling players into a false sense of security, as navigating the city in the day is easy enough, with few serious obstacles in the way. However, come nightfall, players would be faced with a new experience that felt like it was twice as hard.

Techland kept up a relatively constant stream of updates and downloadable content to keep the game relevant and managed to sell more than 16 million copies by 2021.

The sequel faced more criticism for failing to innovate enough in the first game, but *Dying Light* remains a fan favorite.

3. Call of Duty Zombies

There's probably a certain percentage of people who only buy *Call of Duty* nowadays to play the Zombies mode.

First introduced in *Call of Duty: World at War* in 2008 as a mini game called *Nazi Zombies,* it took a couple of months to properly take off or be recognized for what it was. Slowly but surely, though, the mode became far more popular than playing the base game or standard multiplayer.

Zombies' mode is simple. You (and others if played co-op) are in a location. Zombies begin to emerge, intent on killing you. You start on Round 1, and end…never. The game gets progressively more difficult as you play, and you simply see how far you can get before you are totally overwhelmed.

It's simple in concept, but the *CoD* franchise has shown remarkable ingenuity with their Zombies mode, and there have now been several iterations of it. Players and YouTubers obsess over Easter eggs, hacks, and secret tactics that guarantee success. It's come a long way from being a little mini game.

4. Plants vs. Zombies

This will make a few readers feel exceptionally old, but it must be pointed out that there used to be a time when people didn't necessarily do everything with their phones. In the late 2000s, many people with Apple products didn't have an iPhone that did everything. Instead, they may have had an iPod Touch, which was an iPhone but without being a phone, so yes, it was worse.

On May 5, 2009, the infinitely replayable game *Plants vs. Zombies* was released, and many gamers took to their iPod Touches to do battle.

The game is simple. You use plants (with warring capabilities) to destroy zombies who are trying to get into your house. With comedic themes and delightful cartoonish graphics, the game quickly captured the attention of casual gamers and commuters.

Plants vs. Zombies is now a franchise and has full console games to its name. But it was in its relatively simple beginnings that most gamers felt it excelled.

5. Dead Rising

Arguably the most fun game on this list is *Dead Rising*, which was released in 2006 by Capcom.

The game sets you in an American shopping mall, with an open-world environment. Guess what's happened? Yep, there are zombies. Dead Rising's zombies are slow and meandering, but there are tons of them. It's easy to get overwhelmed by the horde quickly, so you have to develop effective strategies to fight your way through the masses.

This is where *Dead Rising* stood out. The game encouraged you to craft strange, improvised weapons to use on the zombies. As you're in a mall, there's a lot to find, and the game allows gamers to use their imagination to best take down the ambling zombies.

Dead Rising really pioneered the use of improvised weapons in gaming and wasn't afraid to add a bit of humor to the zombie apocalypse genre.

6. Dead Island

Released in 2011 by Techland and an obvious precursor to *Dying Light, Dead Island* was a huge success and a game beloved by fans across the world.

The game takes you to a tropical, holiday resort island at the start of a zombie outbreak. Using improvised weaponry and the diverse open world to help you navigate intense levels and masses of zombies, the game was praised for its ambition.

True, *Dead Island* had some serious problems with the consistency of gameplay and had technical issues coming out of its ears. But it was great fun and a follow-up released in 2023 delighted fans, even if some of the old problems persist.

7. Project Zomboid

The 2013 release of *Project Zomboid* is most notable due to its consistent fanbase and the fact that it cost a minute amount compared to the other entries on this list (apart from *Plants vs. Zombies*).

Project Zomboid is a challenging open-world game that is intended to be a simulation of a zombie apocalypse with serious depth and realistic survival mechanics. It quickly developed a community when it was released in early access and has slowly been building from there.

In 2023, *Project Zomboid* has only grown its player base and continues to receive attention and updates from The Indie Stone, its developers.

Gamers eagerly await *Project Zomboid*'s move to console, as it's currently PC-only. The developers are working on it, but it could be some way from being realized.

CHAPTER IV: MODERN CLASSICS

There's no gamer in the 2020s who will read this chapter and just happily say "What a good selection, I don't disagree with any of those."

The term "Modern Classic" is a tough one because the quality of video game production is so high now. Indie titles spend years in development and come out with expertly crafted level design and studios with $50 million budgets produce immersive cinematic experiences at a remarkable pace. Basically, there's an abundance of games that will be a classic for someone.

This chapter features five games that are undeniably classics of the modern era. We're talking game-changing creations, or games that were spoken about the moment they were released and have continued to be spoken about as the years roll by.

If you believe something clear has been missed, don't worry - it's probably featured in another chapter somewhere so you can have a proper fan moment there.

16. THE WITCHER 3: NO HALF-MEASURES

Where else should we start, or could we start, other than here? *The Witcher 3: Wild Hunt* came out in 2015 and quickly won over players with its deep world, rich stories, and attention to detail. The developers at CD Projekt Red helped set the franchise apart from other open-world fantasy games by taking advantage of the chance to add humor and nods to popular culture to the game.

In *The Witcher,* you play as...well, the Witcher. Witchers have unique abilities in monster-slaying and are sought after in the Medievalesque fantasy realm in which the game takes place, as there's a persistent problem with monsters. The problem with releasing a fantasy game in the 2010s is that your competition was a behemoth of video gaming, *Elder Scrolls: Skyrim.*

CD Projekt Red faced the difficult task of distinguishing their game from *Skyrim.* The previous *Witcher* games had their audience but hadn't attracted a gigantic following like the *Elder Scrolls* franchise had managed. The most notable difference that they worked on was to make *Witcher 3*'s combat significantly more fluid than *Skyrim*'s. *Witcher* is a third-person fantasy game, and the pace of the fights with fantastical beasties is far quicker than most battles in competitors' games.

The development team also focused on variety. There is a deep lore within the *Witcher* franchise (just read the *many* books for an idea), so there's lots to draw from. The sheer quantity of monsters in this game is impressive. You face off against so many unique designs that surprise the player in their own way, forcing them to adapt their fighting style as they progress. It's clever and intuitive.

CD Projekt Red, with its work on *Witcher* 3, has managed to preserve its impeccable reputation as a studio, which is tough to do. When a game is immediately very good (or even when it's not - here's looking at you, *No Man's Sky*), it's easy to gain a crowd of loyal followers, but the question is how do you keep them happy?

Some games that fail on release try to update their game quickly, like *No Man's Sky*, to retain the slim audience that's there already. *Witcher 3* was immediately loved, so what do you do to keep it fresh? That's right, release downloadable content that has more in it than most full titles. The sheer effort and backing that CD Projekt Red put into the *Witcher 3* makes it a classic, as any player can pick it up, and start gaming, and it would keep them busy for a year.

The level of detail in the world of *Witcher* further sets it apart from lesser competition. A variety of mission types, excellently written dialogue, and a well-crafted open world provide players with an almost perfect fantasy game.

We could discuss *Witcher 3*'s merits for a further 20,000 words if we wished, but it's better to do that YouTubing thing that was mentioned in the introduction to *see* its appeal for yourself. Or you can smugly sit there and just nod because you have already played it. Now be sad about the fact there's not a *Witcher 4*.

17. POKÉMON GO: EXPLORING THE OUTDOORS

Don't worry, console gamers and hardcore PC gamers that sit there tutting and shaking their heads at the mere mention of *Pokémon Go* in a gaming book.

"That's not a real game!" You cry. Well, cry away. *Pokémon Go* was a phenomenon and undoubtedly a Modern Classic in gaming.

In 2016, *Pokémon Go* exploded onto the mobile gaming scene, drawing in millions of players all over the world with its unique mix of virtual reality and the popular *Pokémon* series. The mobile game urged people to go outside and catch virtual Pokémon with their smartphones. *Pokémon Go* had a big effect on society beyond just being fun. It encouraged people to explore the outdoors, got them moving more, and helped them make friends.

Pokémon Go's unique angle was its interactivity with the players' physical landscape. Unlike most other video games, players had to walk around towns, parks, and other real-world places to find and catch Pokémon. When augmented reality was combined with physical action, players of all ages became more active.

Motivated by the game's goals, many people who hadn't been active before started walking or riding their bikes for long distances to capture Pokémon that had emerged. There aren't many games that can boast of successfully getting gamers into the outside world! Wii Sports tried to get people moving, but we all discovered that you could lie on the sofa with a slice of pizza and just wave the stick around from there.

People playing *Pokémon Go* were urged to interact with their surroundings and find new places. The game's virtual Pokémon were hidden at parks, sites, and other places in the real world, which got people to visit locations they might not have otherwise. This part of the game made people more curious and adventurous, and it turned ordinary walks into exciting hunts for rare Pokémon. If you were somehow not observing the news at the time, you wouldn't have seen the news footage of actual stampedes in New York as people sprinted into Central Park to find a Zapdos. Taking the competition and social aspect of gaming into the real world was inspired - though perhaps annoying for someone trying to enjoy a normal walk in the park!

Pokémon Go showed how virtual reality games could be used to get people all over the world moving, exploring the outdoors, and making new friends. It's been the most successful instance of augmented reality gaming, and perhaps may be the most successful ever. Millions and millions of people downloaded the app in 2016 at its release. Even though the initial excitement died down in 2016, *Pokémon Go* enjoyed a resurgence during the COVID-19 pandemic. When many countries only allowed their citizens to journey outside for a brief period once a day, the game gave people a task in the outside world to accomplish, when so much about ordinary life had been lost.

Pokémon Go was the first game to use augmented reality, and given its huge impact, it deserves recognition as a real classic of the modern era of gaming.

18. HALF-LIFE: THE LONG WAIT FOR A SEQUEL

Creating this chapter requires genuinely difficult choices to be made. But if we're thinking about defining moments in time for the modern gaming era, then it's important to explain the whole, well, hysteria around *Half-Life.*

The *Half-Life* video game series, developed by Valve Corporation, is considered one of the most important franchises in PC gaming history. The series revolutionized first-person shooter (FPS) games and made a significant impact on the gaming industry. *Half-Life* was always ahead of the curve when it came to storytelling, FPS innovations, and character design.

But....

If you ask any fan what you need to know about the creation of *Half-Life*, they'll probably say, "I hate Valve with all of my heart."

Half-Life was released in 1998 and really popularized the concept of a narrative-driven FPS. The game immersed players in its bizarre and immersive storyline, and its graphics were genuinely exceptional for the time. The physics engine made the game intuitive to play, and critics were very impressed.

Then, in 2004, *Half-Life 2* was released to even greater critical reception. The story only developed further, asking more questions, and providing a few answers, but leaving the whole world of *Half-Life* shrouded in mystery still. By this point, as gaming technology was developing, the experience was more cinematic and seamless. Once again, this was accomplished in a way that very few studios had the nerve to attempt at the time.

Valve knew that the fanbase for *Half-Life* wanted the series to have depth and to continue to push boundaries. Valve did this with its Source engine, which further improved graphics, physics, and interactive environments to an impressive degree in the mid-2000s.

We'll take a brief break in detailing the timeline of *Half-Life* here to explain how huge this game really was. Console gamers were frustrated at the PC community that had built around the game, while the gaming community began to ask questions like, "Is this the best gaming franchise of all time?" Seriously!

Half-Life was a strong influence on titles like *Bioshock* and *Metro 2033,* in which horror elements blurred the lines between genres. The Source engine also laid the groundwork for *Portal,* which really could have been on this list itself for its pure ingenuity, and *Team Fortress 2,* a genuine online craze in the late 2000s. *Half-Life 1* and *2* had proven that gamers could handle more and wanted more when it came to games. Fans eagerly awaited the next installment.

This came a few years later in 2007 with *Half-Life 2: Episode Two,* the first part of a trilogy of episodic sequels to *Half-Life 2.* Valve announced that they would be producing shorter, frequent content updates to the story and fans should be prepared for this new form of episodic gaming for the series. *Half-Life 2: Episode Two* was a great gaming experience for fans but ended on a cliffhanger. That's not a problem though, because surely an installment would be just around the corner, right? After all, that's what Valve said…

Wrong!

It would be *13 years* before a new *Half-Life* game was released!

The long wait was torture for fans of *Half-Life*. Valve continued to produce games and developed their revolutionary PC gaming platform *Steam,* which has absolutely dominated how PC games are played and sold. Every time there was to be "an announcement," fans would eagerly tune in and demand, "Announce *Half-Life* 3!"

No announcement came for years, then quite suddenly there *was* an announcement and release of *Half-Life: Alyx* in March 2020. The game was not a sequel to *Half-Life* 2, however; in fact, it was set before that point. But *Alyx* was a potentially transformative project that we're still living in the effects of it.

Alyx was a virtual reality game and featured unbelievable levels of detail. VR games have been developing for the last decade, moving from simple point-and-click adventures, to…, well, *Alyx*. The game's setting and plot were unbelievably detailed - and exceptionally impressive. So impressive that a math teacher was able to teach a lesson to their pupils by using chalk that actually worked like chalk in the game!

Alyx has shown the potential of VR gaming and who knows what other projects are in development for this emerging technology because of *Alyx*'s impressive release.

Fans are still waiting, however, for *Half-Life 3* and a continuation of the story. The series is an undoubted modern classic entirely because the fans are so feverish for more of its gaming content. Any news about *Half-Life* is massive and is the biggest news in the community. It doesn't matter whether Valve simply says, "We're working on the series" or "Nothing is imminent," the words are analyzed and pulled apart, so desperate are gamers for more *Half-Life*.

Maybe *Half-Life 3* will be released soon…sometime in the next 200 years or so!

19. THE LAST OF US: MASTERY IN STORYTELLING

Oh look, it's the one that was left out of the Zombie bit of the Horror chapter.

When we think of Modern Gaming classics, you can't really look much further than *The Last of Us*, which was released in 2013 by Naughty Dog. Naughty Dog was also responsible for the *Uncharted* series mentioned earlier, and *Crash Bandicoot*, which unfortunately has narrowly missed a mention in this book but is an exceptional title. The reason we're mentioning Naughty Dog's other successes is to impress on you the point that they *do not miss*.

Naughty Dog has been creating generation-defining PlayStation games for 25 years now and may have just created their *magnum opus* with *The Last of Us*.

The Last of Us and *The Last of Us II* are zombie games on the surface. That didn't exactly set them up to be instant classics as the genre is worn-out and saturated. However, this game separated itself from that massive herd in three main ways: the writing, the graphics, and the acting.

If you ask someone who's played both *Last of Us* games and ask them what they enjoyed the most, they will point to the story. Broadly speaking, the plot focuses on Joel and Ellie, who journey through the apocalyptic wasteland of America to complete quests, unraveling aspects of underground fighting and government corruption along the way. Ellie is a teenage girl while Joel is an ex-father who lost his daughter during the outbreak of the virus. The virus is a type of adaptive fungus that takes over people and turns them into vile zombified creatures, sickening even seasoned horror fans with their grotesque design.

The writing in the games is second to none, and that is meant literally. You'd be hard-pressed to find a game that's better written and devised than *The Last of Us*. The story is just perfect. Players are drawn into a troubled relationship on the micro-level, focused on Joel's hardened exterior that crumbles in the face of the likeable Ellie, while we watch her sharpen and become a formidable character in this unforgiving new world. On the macro-level, we invest in how America has crumbled, rather than overcome, and how society limps on. It's multi-layered, intriguing, fun, and devastating. Also, there are zombies.

Graphically, the *Last of Us* has shown what's possible for the PlayStation 4 and then the PlayStation 5. The game is crushingly realistic in what it's trying to depict. There's no crazy battle between Gods going on, nor time travel through a black hole to contend with. The developers therefore had to ground the game in reality and fully realize the broken world that confronts the player. The result is a meticulously detailed environment and startlingly lifelike character movements that increase the necessary buy-in from the player.

Of course, you can have a good script, but without good acting, the project will fail artistically. The gaming world abounds with examples of this. Just look at the recent *Gollum* game as one example (though that also failed because of the graphics, plot, gameplay, concept, price-point, writing, acting, development, response to criticism, and every other metric).

Troy Baker as Joel and Ashley Johnson as Ellie provide flawless performances in their roles, which can be difficult when one isn't physically acting. There are no dud lines, no - "Oh, we'll go with that take because we haven't got time." Naughty Dog gave the space for the actors to properly figure out the characters and bring them to life. There's a reason that *The Last of Us* is one of the only examples of a successful game adaptation into a movie or TV series. It was easier for them to make it because the game was perfectly scripted already.

The Last of Us is a modern classic, plain and simple. If you haven't played it (and are over 18) then put this book down, go and play it, have a little cry, and then come back.

Done that? Good, let's continue.

20. CALL OF DUTY: MASTERING ONLINE MULTIPLAYER

"Hated, adored, never ignored." So goes the mantra of Manchester United fans around the world and as applicable as it is to a colossal soccer franchise, it's also applicable to the biggest FPS game series of all time.

Call of Duty started in 2003 as a World War II shooter developed by Infinity Ward. The first three games laid the foundation of intuitive FPS controls, creative map design, and the start of online battles. *Call of Duty III* was really where this was truly realized. It's important to remember that, before 2007, online multiplayer wasn't as competent and universal as it is nowadays. In the 2020s, 99% of games have some sort of online aspect to them, even if it's not a multiplayer battle-style game. Why do we say, "before 2007," you ask?

Well, in 2007 Infinity Ward brought out *Call of Duty 4: Modern Warfare* and changed the future of gaming. No exaggeration, 2007 was the year that online gaming blossomed. That's not to say it wouldn't have done so without *Call of Duty* - it would have, certainly - but Infinity Ward showed the world what could be done by keeping it simple.

Modern Warfare introduced a progressive system, where you leveled up through a series of objectives, achievements, and XP gained through fighting online against other players. It was basic but perfect. You won points online and progressed up the levels, gaining access to new weapons as you did so, before you then had the option to "Prestige," giving up your weaponry for a special cosmetic that let all the other players know how wonderful you are at shooting them in the head.

How often do we see this model now? The basic concept is copied across driving games, FPSs, open-world games, and all sorts: Play it lots and gain access to the stuff that the others don't get to.

Call of Duty releases a new game every year, with Treyarch also providing games for the franchise, and every year it sells outrageously well. Several entries will sell millions of copies within the first 24 hours, and it is one of the most commercially successful franchises of all time. This isn't to say the quality has always remained the same. *Modern Warfare* may have been a near-perfect multiplayer experience but *Call of Duty: Ghosts* turned many away from the franchise due to its horrible..., everything.

Still, the series occupies the top spot in the FPS genre and shows no sign of giving up. It remains the dominant game for casual online play, and constantly adapts its time and location to keep the games somewhat fresh. It also doesn't seem to matter how many players sign out of the franchise, stop taking part, or just grow out of it. There's always a new crop ready to take their place.

DID YOU KNOW: MINECRAFT

Minecraft, or *Minceraft* if you've been lucky enough to spot it, was officially released in 2011. It is important to say "officially" because *Minecraft* was being played for years before its release in Alpha and Beta form.

Minecraft is another game with a simple concept. In a blocky world that is procedurally generated, your blocky character has to survive by harvesting materials from its environment and building things with them. The game has no end and at its release, no story. *Minecraft* is a "sandbox" game. Like kids in a sandbox, players are free to do whatever they want within it.

Everyone has heard of *Minecraft.* Even the cave-dwelling, subterranean amoeba that has gone unchanged since 25,000,000 BCE understand what a Creeper is. But there are many fascinating aspects of *Minecraft* that you may be unaware of, so here's a very small snapshot of the game that puts a massive nerd into a house in Beverly Hills.

1. *Minecraft* is a creation of video game developer "Notch," whose real name is Markus Persson, and made by Mojang

Studios. Notch created *Minecraft* out of his childhood love for LEGO, finding its endless creativity inspiring. He initially looked to create a space-themed game but settled on the sandbox nature of *Minecraft*.

2. *Minecraft* was released in *Alpha* in 2010. This was odd for the time; games weren't generally sold for play until they were fully ready or maybe in *Beta* from time to time. Alpha refers to an earlier stage in development, and such games are normally full of bugs and problems to be fixed. Selling the game in *Alpha* was a bold move but proved ingenious. Millions flocked to buy the earlier forms of the game, with some gamers nostalgically pointing to the *Alpha* years being the best years of *Minecraft*.

3. The recognizable enemy of the "Creeper" is about 50% accidental in design. The creature wasn't meant to hiss and explode, but for some reason it did. So, Notch decided that it was a pretty formidable enemy, and should stay walking around, blowing up in the face of the player. Thanks, Notch.

4. In 2014, Notch decided to buy himself a house. Why not, the game had been a moderate success. Notch purchased a $70m mansion in Beverly Hills, LA, outbidding Beyonce and Jay-Z in the process. This was only a few years after *Alpha*, and he already had enough money to buy that house! Talk about a meteoric rise. He later sold the house to Jay-Z and Beyonce after he decided to move away. Now Notch's net worth is well over a billion dollars, helped by Microsoft's acquisition of Mojang, the company that produced *Minecraft*, for $2.5 billion. All that from playing with LEGO as a kid and having an overactive imagination…

5. *Minecraft*'s timing was impeccable. When it hit *Alpha,* YouTube was one of the most visited sites in the world and gaming YouTube was just taking off. The gaming side of YouTube is interesting; it's mainly just people playing games while talking over the top of the vision, but people love watching it. *Minecraft* attracted great interest on YouTube because you could do anything in it. This helped it spread rapidly, and we're talking *rapidly*. YouTubers like Yogscast helped Minecraft (and themselves) become the most talked about gaming property on the planet within two years.
6. *Minecraft* has become an educational tool. Teachers and researchers across the world have been investigating the impact of free creativity in the classroom, and whether the game may be widely used in schools. LEGO has been involved in the same studies, and what is *Minecraft* if not 3D Lego?
7. Thank your lucky stars that it's called *Minecraft*; initially, it was going to be called *Cave Game,* which may have placed it as the worst-named game ever after *Fishing Simulator 2014*. If you're lucky enough to spot it when you log in, the title screen will read *Minceraft* instead of *Minecraft*. There's about a 0.01% chance of that happening, but it's a joy when it does.

There are tons to talk about with *Minecraft,* but that's just a few "did you know" facts for you. Happy mining!

CHAPTER V: FANTASTICAL FEATURES

The Fantasy genre is a bit of a weird one because aren't all video games "fantasy" to some degree? We don't come home from work, eager for rest, and then play a game about being at a boring job. Well, gamers of *Euro Truck Simulator 2022* do, but they're a strange bunch who should be admired for their dedication to spending their recreational time doing something so dull.

Fantasy really means gaming in a world that isn't your own, one that's completely removed or completely different, or it might only have a few key differences. Either way, it's about placing your being in an arena that is not possible.

In this chapter, we'll look at games that are either part of the Fantasy genre or have fantastical elements. Allow your mind to wander into otherworldly landscapes or just a well-decorated five-bedroom house.

21. FINAL FANTASY: CASUAL GAMING DISCOURAGED

Marmite, the strange yeasty spread from the United Kingdom has the slogan, "You love it, or you hate it" as their marketing strategy. Ignoring the fact that it is oh-so-British to tell people that they may not actually like the product, the same notion applies to the *Final Fantasy* series. Though, admittedly it's more aptly, "You either get it or you don't."

In the realm of video games, few series have reigned so supreme for decades, enchanting players with their epic narratives, fantastical worlds, and groundbreaking innovation, like *Final Fantasy*. Developed by Square Enix (formerly Square), the first *Final Fantasy* game was released on December 18, 1987, in Japan, laying the foundation for a legendary franchise that continues to captivate gamers around the globe.

The *Final Fantasy* series weaves tales of heroism, love, and sacrifice across various mystical realms, full of a unique cast of characters and magical beings. Through innovative gameplay mechanics, cinematic storytelling, and awe-inspiring visuals, *Final Fantasy* has left an indelible mark on the gaming landscape.

The series attracts millions who wish to escape to high fantasy worlds that are intrinsically linked yet far removed from our own.

Final Fantasy's impact on gaming is attributed to its genre-defining features. All fantasy games owe their existence to *Final Fantasy* in some way, and many games have happily adopted features from the series to further the depth of their experience.

The series revolutionized the role-playing game (RPG) genre by introducing intricate storylines and character development, elevating video game narratives to the level of epic fantasy novels. RPG elements are now seen in almost all video games. Sports games have career modes that involve progression and role-playing, while 99% of notable action games feature some sort of progression tree that enables you to learn moves. Even horror games have taken it on. The RPG element is almost necessary to make your game stand a chance in today's world of gaming, whereby players *want* to buy in, and this is really thanks to *Final Fantasy*.

Final Fantasy also popularized the turn-based combat system, where players take turns to execute commands during battles. This tactical approach to combat set the benchmark for many RPGs that followed, and still has its place in the more technologically advanced scene of the 2020s. The revered *South Park* RPG games utilize turn-based strategy to great effect, while the *Pokémon* franchise almost universally adopts turn-based combat in their games. *Final Fantasy* has, on occasion, moved away from this system, but it's a fan favorite and Square Enix has further innovated on the idea, making it more seamless in later titles.

As of 2021, the *Final Fantasy* series has sold over 179 million units worldwide, becoming one of the best-selling video game franchises in history. The series' popularity has transcended gaming, with numerous novels, manga, anime adaptations, and even a feature film, *Final Fantasy VII: Advent Children*.

With over 30 mainline titles and numerous spin-offs, the *Final Fantasy* franchise demonstrates remarkable versatility, appealing to players of different ages and gaming preferences. Square Enix has made sure to move the series with the times. The games have successfully adapted to changing technology and platforms, from their origins on the NES to the modern era of consoles, PCs, and mobile devices.

Final Fantasy's innovations in the RPG and Fantasy genres are felt in almost every dark recess of gaming. Almost all genres now include some version of *Final Fantasy*'s progression system through levelling up, move-learning, XP building, party management, and the other areas of innovation that the series brought. The games aren't for everyone but in a good way. The series has never compromised on its often-bizarre vision for the sake of popularity, instead letting the fans come to them.

22. STAR WARS: CRAFTING LEGENDARY GAMING STATUS

Of course, *Star Wars* isn't known most commonly as a gaming staple. It is known as a sci-fi movie series first, TV series second, and then as a video game franchise. But some of the *Star Wars* video games made a huge impact on the Fantasy gaming genre, with a few games reaching a legendary status among the gamers who remember their release (sorry to make some of you feel old).

Star Wars had an immediate impact as a movie franchise. George Lucas put frankly astonishing levels of effort into the early films, building up a galaxy of civilizations, war, and characters - all of which were crying out for a decent video game adaptation. They got several. The *Star Wars* video games have traversed diverse genres, including action-adventure, role-playing, space combat, strategy, and more. Throughout the years, players have embarked on heroic quests, epic space battles, and thrilling lightsaber duels, all set against the backdrop of the iconic *Star Wars* universe.

It's difficult to know where to start, so let's begin with a small run down of those legendary titles.

First, the *Knights of the Old Republic* or *KOTOR*, which was released in 2003 by BioWare. *KOTOR* stands as a critically acclaimed role-playing game, praised for its deep story, moral choices, and rich lore. *KOTOR* is still referenced well into the 2020s by gamers who grew up in the early 2000s. The RPG system was impeccably crafted, and many felt it was a perfect *Star Wars* game. There are continuous calls for a remaster, as is the fashion in 2020s gaming, and it retains an exceptional rating on Steam, where it can be purchased.

The clear favorite of console players was *Star Wars: Battlefront II*, released by Pandemic Studios in 2005. If there's a Video Game Hall of Fame, then *Battlefront II* is one of the shoe-ins for it. This action-packed shooter was celebrated for its intense multiplayer battles and iconic locations. Despite its troubled launch, the game achieved cult status for its addictive gameplay and vast content. In 2005, it was one of the few games that was able to boast online multiplayer, which was unreliable (come on, it was 2005) but special. The game received a sort of re-release in the late 2010s but failed to attract the same reception.

What's better than *Star Wars*? *Star Wars* in LEGO. The LEGO video games are in another sphere really and are fantastic. They successfully managed to make a game that's "easy to grasp, hard to master," and is a favorite for families across the world. The *Star Wars* iterations were loved and laid the foundation for further LEGO games later. You offer anyone the chance to play co-op with you on any *LEGO: Star Wars* game, and you've got a six-hour session incoming.

Unfortunately, not all, *Star Wars* games have been created equally, and there have been some that were borderline disasters. We won't spend long on this, but here's a quick rundown of the games in the franchise that didn't do so well.

Star Wars: The Force Unleashed was released in 2008 and while praised for its action and story, it faced criticism for boring gameplay and lackluster character development. The reboot of *Battlefront* in 2015 was heavily criticized for its lack of single-player content (a staple of the beloved *Battlefront II*) and poor depth of gameplay. At its release it had such a limited number of maps for multiplayer gaming that many demanded a refund; some gamers even threatened to sue (but they were very dramatic). *Battlefront II* was released a few years later and made significant improvements on these failures, to EA's credit.

When *Star Wars* gets it right, it gets it very right. The universe has only been emboldened by the successes of *KOTOR* and *Battlefront*; the video game galaxy has been an epic journey of success and challenges. From legendary titles that captured the essence of the *Star Wars* universe to games that faced criticism, each entry has contributed to the enduring legacy of *Star Wars* in gaming. As the journey continues, fans eagerly anticipate future experiences that will transport them to a galaxy far, far away, where the Force and gaming innovation combine to create memorable adventures.

23. SAMUS ARAN: BREAKING STEREOTYPES OF BADASSES

Samus Aran, the protagonist of Nintendo's *Metroid* series, stands out in the annuals of gaming. As one of the first female protagonists in video game history, her character shattered gender stereotypes in gaming.

Samus Aran entered the scene in the original *Metroid* game in 1986, an era when most video game characters were male. Samus is a heavily armored character who faces off against adversaries against a sci-fi backdrop. The decision to make Samus a woman was made late in development, with the developers wanting to surprise players who would assume the armored character was male. This surprise was revealed only at the end of the game, and only if certain conditions were met, leading to a memorable and defining moment in gaming history.

Samus's character was heavily influenced by the *Alien* films and its protagonist, Ellen Ripley, played by Sigourney Weaver. Just as Ripley was a strong, independent character battling terrifying alien creatures, so too was Samus. This influence extended to the

Metroid creatures themselves, which share a similar life cycle to the Xenomorphs of the *Alien* franchise. This influence doesn't stop there. Samus's Power Suit, a piece of Chozo technology that she wears, also shares some design elements with the space suits seen in the *Alien* films, with its bold colors, sharp lines, and intimidating visor.

Like many early video game characters, Samus was traditionally a silent protagonist, her thoughts and motivations were left up to the player's interpretation. This all changed with the release of *Metroid: Other M* in 2010, where Samus was voiced by actress Jessica Martin, to a mixed reception from dedicated fans.

The *Metroid* games maintain a loyal fanbase, some of whom were there at the start of the franchise in 1986. For many of Nintendo's gamers, Samus is best known for her appearance in every *Super Smash Bros.* game to date and has two forms: her armored form and her Zero Suit form, the latter of which shows her without her Power Suit.

Samus Aran, with her unexpected reveal and compelling design, changed the landscape of gaming by proving that a female character could lead a successful action game. Her influence extends beyond the *Metroid* series, as she paved the way for more diverse character representation in the world of video games.

24. THE SIMS: SIMULATION AND LIVING LIFE

Now look, *The SIMS* isn't high fantasy like *Final Fantasy* or galactic opera like *Star Wars*. But it's a different type of fantasy game - have you seen how expensive housing is nowadays?!

Joking aside, *SIMS* is a game series about working to craft a great life and home for a person or family of your creation. The games have been produced by Electronic Arts, or EA, since 2000 and have been immensely popular since their release. As technology has improved, gamers' choices in *SIMS* have improved too. The choices available in the first *SIMS* game pale in comparison to the plethora of home improvement options in the more recent *SIMS 4*.

SIMS offers different avenues of play in their games. Some gamers are happiest creating houses and populating their neighborhood with viable living options for the AI-controlled SIMS. Others like to create one SIM, possibly in their image, and control them to start a family, upgrade their living quarters, and work the job of their dreams.

The SIMS themselves offer a unique gaming experience. Whichever SIM the gamer controls will happily obey the instructions given by the gamer, who works as an omnipotent creator and dictator. Amusingly though, the SIMS also operate in a distinct fourth wall-breaking fashion, loudly complaining into the empty sky toward the gamer if a basic need is forgotten. These sorts of interactions keep the game fresh and entertaining. While *SIMS* offers simulation and fantasy, it's designed to be cartoonish in feel and offer soft-play levels of entertainment for most age groups.

The games have held a wide appeal over time, and an exceptionally loyal customer base, occasionally to a fault. *The SIMS 3* faced criticism for the baffling number of extensions and purchasable additions available. Players could spend hundreds of dollars on add-ons without technically having access to the "full game."

The appeal of *The SIMS* is easy to see: it's pure fantasy. Either gamers are luxuriating in an unachievable life as a movie star living in a mansion, or a more chilled-out gardener with a small position in a café, working toward that new dining room table. It's an escape from the trials of real life through a life that's simpler and easier to succeed in. Some people, however, enjoy torturing their SIMS, and who's to say that's wrong? In the early days, players discovered that murdering your SIM is surprisingly easy, either by locking them in a burning room, removing the ladder to the swimming pool, or simply starving them to death..., it's all good. If you do it enough, then SIMS can become friends with Death, the character, and he'll start coming over for parties.

SIMS is an enduring game because of its fantastical elements, allowing people to experience a separate life from their own. Each new game continues to develop in features and precise customization, and players revel in the increasingly detailed worlds that they can become lost in.

25. GOD OF WAR: REPACKAGING THE PAST FOR THE PRESENT

You don't get much more fantastical than the *God of War* series. The games follow the character of Kratos who, starting as a Greek civilian, is transformed into a monster-like brute who becomes known across human mythology for killing Gods. *God of War* is epic, grand, gruesome, and hilariously fun. "Kratos" comes from a minor god in Greek mythology, but his personality is very different from that God; he is driven by fury at the Gods who manipulated him into slaughtering his family. The rage that Kratos draws from is inspired by Edward Norton's character in *American History X*, a man whose intense rage destroys his life and close relationships. Kratos was created at Santa Monica Studio by David Jaffe, and designed as such because the creators wanted to make a character who was cruel and not a standard hero.

The first games of *God of War* were beat-'em-up-style games, filled with constant fighting and bloody destruction. Kratos journeyed across Roman and Greek mythology, contesting the flawed, evil Gods that ruled those realms. While in these worlds,

Kratos is a younger man driven by fury, and that's echoed by the style of gameplay. Nothing comes between Kratos and his goal. His impossible levels of strength ultimately best everyone he comes up against, leading to a series of impressively unique and grotesque deaths for those he encounters.

There was a period of silence for the *God of War* games after the release of *God of War III* in 2010. Kratos had bested the Roman and Greek pantheon, and many gamers considered the series to be done. It would be considered a fun series but of the time. "Button mashing" games like *God of War* were falling out of vogue. The more considered combat displayed in games such as *Arkham Asylum* and *Assassin's Creed* was becoming more desirable and satisfying, while the storyline seemed to be at a natural end.

That was until 2016 when Santa Monica dropped a now famous, secret gameplay trailer at the E3 convention. Go and watch it on YouTube if you haven't seen it already. The moment that Kratos is unveiled, out of nowhere, as a now older man with a huge beard is fantastic. The E3 crowd starts screaming - so few people had expected there to be a new *God of War* and now we have OLD *God of War*?!

This was the reboot of the franchise and marked a departure from past games. Now Kratos was based on Norse mythology, a rich and complex series of tales of apocalypse and troubled Gods, and he had a son. *God of War* (2018) and *God of War: Ragnarok* (2022) showed a considered Kratos, who had reflected on the mistakes and fury of his past. This older God is wary of confrontation and desperate to keep his son safe and secure in their home in the forest. Of course, that doesn't happen, and Kratos instead embarks on a twisting, turning journey that sees him battle against the demons of his past and the constant threat of Gods in the present.

The newer *God of War* games received exceptional reviews and a bounty of awards with their releases; the whole franchise has seen a new breath of life and a new generation of gamers excited to see what's coming next. The aging of Kratos helped retain the older fans, who had also grown. Long gone were the teenagers of the late 2000s who just wanted to see as much blood as possible; they now needed something more to grapple with.

Though the series has changed in style, *God of War* holds its own as an emotional and epic fantastical story that explores all depths of human emotion. Santa Monica has drawn on ancient myths to create a truly unique series that must be played to be believed.

DID YOU KNOW: KINGDOM HEARTS

We have already discussed *Final Fantasy* in this book, and this 'Did You Know' will focus on the closely linked *Kingdom Hearts*.

Kingdom Hearts is a game franchise that marries Square Enix characters (i.e., *Final Fantasy*) and Disney characters in an RPG. The first *Kingdom Hearts* game was released in 2002 and offered players a blend of action and role-playing elements. Its story centers around Sora, a young boy who becomes a Keyblade wielder; Donald Duck, a feisty but loyal magician; and Goofy, the lovable, clumsy knight. Their journey through various Disney worlds to defeat the malevolent Heartless and find their friends Riku and Kairi forms the crux of the story.

The series is beloved by fans and boasts 13 titles across multiple platforms, with future titles planned. You may have a few questions about the franchise, so here is a small "Did You Know" section about this fantastical and unique series.

1. *Kingdom Hearts* was conceived in an elevator, a Square Enix producer and a Disney producer happened to bump into each other and got talking. The meeting led to bigger meetings and

more executives, and before too long, the companies had agreed to collaborate on a series of video games.

2. Disney should thank Square Enix for pushing the project, as it was Mickey Mouse's first outing as a playable character in a video game. It would not be his last, and Disney games have gone on to sell well across the planet, with Mickey featuring in many.

3. The name *Kingdom Hearts* was decided upon as it was felt that it encapsulated the two companies perfectly. "Kingdom" was representative of the various Disney worlds that were visited, while "Hearts" symbolized the emotional depth of the storyline, characteristic of *Final Fantasy*. The charming appearance of *Kingdom Hearts* is just the surface of these games; the director Tetsuya Nomura wrote an intricate plot into the series focusing on themes of love, friendship, and the fight between good and evil. The experience was a surprise for video game critics at the time, most of whom assumed that *Kingdom Hearts* was a silly collaboration that wouldn't stand the test of time.

4. Square Enix recognized the necessity to lean into the Disney aesthetic as much as possible. They worked tirelessly to realize many famous locations from Disney movies such as *Pirates of the Caribbean, Frozen, Toy Story, Hercules,* and *Nightmare Before Christmas*. The studio also went to great lengths to secure the original voices behind fan favorites such as Hades, Ariel, and Donald Duck. Gamers weren't used to seeing decent renditions of Disney in a video game and it helped with the franchise's appeal.

Kingdom Hearts is praised as much for its bizarre nature as for the gameplay and story. It's such a weird leap of imagination, to marry the two universes together, and it's that exact weird leap that made it such a success. Thank goodness for that chance encounter in an elevator!

CHAPTER VI: COMPUTER CREATIONS

As we pass the halfway point of the book, our attention turns to computer games. Of course, most games are often referred to as "computer games," but here we mean gaming moments that are mainly played ON a computer or are closely linked to the computer.

Computer gamers have an odd reputation among the wider community. For years, the debate between XBOX and PlayStation has raged, with the different sides coming to blows over the small differences in the console wars. Meanwhile, the computer gamer looks on, smugly happy with their gaming tower - which they may have built themselves - that can run any game better than any console.

Admittedly, it cost them five times as much to put together, but there we go.

Computer gamers are often the boundary pushers anyway. It's easier for them to manipulate game files than on the consoles, and there is usually a greater variety of video games available for the computer. Older games like *Warcraft 3* and *Rollercoaster*

Tycoon still maintain a strong community that maintains and updates the games with innovative modding far beyond what is found in the console realm.

Here are a few notable computer gaming highlights to get to grips with. Just make sure you brush the Cheeto dust off your fingers first, please.

26. BINDING OF ISAAC: A GAME ABOUT…. I BEG YOUR PARDON.

In 2010, Edmund McMillen was a game creator who had recently achieved some recognition for his excellent side-scroller *Super Meat Boy*. McMillen was known in the gaming world for his weirdly excellent imagination and clever mastery of a simple project. McMillen created games that were in the Flash style, software that was heavily used in the 2000s to make computer games.

In 2011, he released *The Binding of Isaac* on Steam to very little fanfare or recognition.

*The Binding of Isaac (TBOI)*went on to become McMillen's best-selling game and is still going strong across PlayStation, PC, XBOX, and Nintendo, boasting an impressive amount of content.

TBOI was conceived by McMillen and co-creator Florian Himsl in a week-long game jam. They spent time together, put their creative minds to work, and hashed out a game that was set to explore McMillen's conflicted opinion on his religious upbringing and the positives and negatives that came from that. What was released was a thoughtful, philosophical exploration of the dichotomy of good and evil, and about our path through our time on Earth.

Only joking, what came was a complete nightmare that sold more than five million games by 2015!

TBOI is a game where you play as a baby. The baby's mother receives a demented message from God, who tells her to kill her baby. The baby escapes to the basement, where it battles all kinds of vile monsters with its tears, as it is constantly crying. The monsters have religious themes at times, some are simply gross, and the items you pick up along the way are best described as sickeningly bizarre. Yep, *TBOI* is weird.

The game is a roguelike game, based on the first *Legend of Zelda*'s dungeon structure. In essence, McMillen wanted to create what amounted to a homage to the beloved classic - the positive reviews and massive sales indicate that he succeeded.

As you may be able to work out, this game attracted controversy. Some outraged video game fans said the title was tantamount to blasphemy, while others applauded its strange exploration of religion as a force for good and bad. However, overwhelmingly, the critics and fans loved it. The game is randomly generated upon every playthrough, meaning that the gamer has a unique experience every time. Items synergize with each other in strange, wonderful ways, and players are left to do their best with what they've got.

After the Flash software left little chance for expansion to consoles in 2014, McMillen began working on a more polished version of the game that added massive amounts of content and was less prone to random crashes. In November of that year, *The Binding of Isaac: Rebirth* was released on PC, Linux, PlayStation, XBOX, Mac, and Nintendo, and it has gone on to have two expansions, plus a very loyal fanbase.

TBOI is an unsettling game with horror and RPG elements that slowly reveal a disturbing story from the mind of Edmund McMillen. Its success is almost entirely down to its infinite replay-ability. Gamers pour *hundreds* of hours into the series, vastly outstripping the time invested in other major game series, because of the randomness of the experience. Now a legendary indie title that more than holds its own in the history of PC gaming, it truly must be seen to be believed.

27. MICROSOFT EXCEL 95: THE HALL OF TORTURED SOULS

Easter eggs have been a part of video games for a long time, but sometimes they show up in software that seems normal, or plain. The spreadsheet tool Microsoft Excel 95 had a hidden gem that made it stand out and provided some form of entertainment to bored office workers. The unusual Easter egg made the work tool into an unexpected mini game in the style of *Doom* called *The Hall of Tortured Souls*.

Microsoft Excel 95 came out in 1995 and was mostly a spreadsheet program. It gave users a variety of tools for organizing and analyzing data - it was on 98% of office computers at the time. But a group of Microsoft programmers saw a chance to add a bit of surprise to the software. At the time, video games were very popular and were only becoming more popular, so they decided to add a secret mini game as a fun Easter egg to give users a break from their spreadsheet work.

Users of Microsoft Excel 95 had to take a very specific set of steps to get to *The Hall of Tortured Souls*. By starting a new workbook, going to cell reference "ROW," typing "95," and then holding down the "Shift" key while clicking on the "Help" menu and choosing "About Microsoft Excel," users could make a hidden game screen similar to that of *Doom* appear. Then, players could look around a digital place called *The Hall of Tortured Souls*.

The Hall of Tortured Souls was a dark, maze-like scene that reminded people of first-person shooter games. The walls were covered with scary pictures and words, such as the names of the people who worked on Microsoft Excel 95. The mini game wasn't as complicated or exciting to play as a full-fledged video game, but it was a fun surprise in an otherwise boring software program.

The Hall of Tortured Souls had no direct effect on Excel's main features, it just added a bit of a surprise and fun for users who came across it. It also showed how software is made with a human touch.

Even though *The Hall of Tortured Souls* may not be as well known to the general public as an Easter egg in video games, it has gained a strong following among fans. With the rise of the internet, more people learned about the Easter egg because people could share what they found and help others find the secret mini game. *The Hall of Tortured Souls* demonstrates that secret surprises can be found in the strangest of places, making software users more curious and encouraging them to look around.

28. MINESWEEPER AND SOLITAIRE: THE SOLUTION AND CAUSE OF BOREDOM AT WORK

Do not scoff, you young whippersnappers! *Solitaire* and *Minesweeper* are two classic computer games that have been bundled with Microsoft's Windows operating system since the early days and have had a surprisingly positive impact on the gaming industry. Despite being simple and relatively low-tech, these games have left a lasting mark on gamers and the gaming landscape.

Solitaire and *Minesweeper* came pre-installed on millions of Windows PCs and were first included as part of the operating system in 1990. Solitaire is a card game from the 19th century, and the version on the Windows PC was designed to help people get used to operating Windows, as well as using a computer mouse. *Minesweeper* is a deceptively difficult game that was created for the same reasons and caused many people to "rage quit" for the first time.

Unbeknownst to the players, these games introduced casual gaming to a vast audience, including people who might not have considered themselves gamers. As a result, these games became some of the most widely played video games in history, reaching players across different age groups and demographics. For many people, *Solitaire* and Minesweeper *were* their first experiences with using a computer mouse and navigating a graphical user interface. These games played a crucial role in familiarizing users with basic computer skills, making them feel comfortable using technology.

These games served as perfect time-fillers during work breaks, study sessions, or moments of downtime. Their straightforward gameplay and lack of complex narratives made them ideal stress relievers and distractions, earning them a special place in the hearts of office workers and students alike. There's still a market for the "pick-up-and-put-down" style of casual gaming that *Solitaire* and *Minesweeper* offered. Arguably, they were the first successful casual gaming experience that didn't take up too much time or concentration.

Minesweeper and *Solitaire* are still widely played on many devices, no longer restricted to the Windows operating system. Many versions are available on free gaming websites, game consoles, Steam, and on any mobile phone. Almost everyone has some sort of connection to the games (particularly if they're 25 and over) and can recall a time that they got *really* into one of them, before deciding that they shouldn't give their life over to a simple game that dates back to 1990.

29. GARRY'S MOD: LOOKING INTO THE MIND OF THE GAMER – AND WISHING WE HADN'T!

Garry's Mod, or GMod as it's often abbreviated, was developed by the British game designer Garry Newman in 2004. It was designed to be a mod for *Half-Life* 2, and its purpose is to allow players to have full control over a virtual environment through object manipulation, physics control, and scenario creation. GMod grew in popularity rapidly, mostly because of its open-ended nature. Players could create movies, game levels, or anything they wanted using the game. Games that offer this much creative control to gamers are often popular, as we can see through the success of open-ended games like *SIMS* and *Minecraft.*

Naturally, GMod has received lots of modding from amateur and professional game designers over the years. Gamers' favorite characters and environments have been rendered in GMod, providing fans with even more fun in creating their environments.

Gamers are an interesting bunch, particularly those who are into modding and spending hours creating their own scenarios in-game. Garry's Mod rose in popularity at the same time that YouTube became a dominant form of entertainment on the internet. This, of course, led to a surge in amateur animations carried out through Garry's Mod. There is now a plethora of surprisingly innovative movies and music videos made using GMod and an equal amount of frankly disturbing, bizarre clips that rely on having an encyclopedic knowledge of gaming culture to even begin to understand.

Garry's Mod is a tool that gamers can use to create whatever comes to their minds and to make the *exact* game that they want to play, and for that it is irreplaceable. GMod creators helped popularize game modes such as *Prop Hunt, Trouble in Terrorist Town*, and *Sandbox*, with *Prop Hunt* now a popular inclusion in many gaming franchises such as *Call of Duty*.

GMod holds a soft spot in many hearts for giving players the chance to throw away objectives and simply enjoy being silly. It's difficult to summarize why it's important or significant because it's difficult to summarize *what* it is. The best way to describe it is as a community experience. At its best, it provides space for anyone to play the games they want in their own way, which makes it special for many gamers.

30. TOTAL WAR: BRINGING THE HISTORY CHANNEL TO YOUR COMPUTER

Q: Who are the only people who are more insufferable nerds than hardcore gamers?

A: Historians.

So, what happens when you combine the two? Well, you get a series of games that provide a semi-realistic historical battle for you to enjoy (if you love history and real-time strategy).

This game is the *Total War* franchise, which has been going strong since 2000 when the first game, *Shogun: Total War,* was developed by Creative Assembly. *Shogun* was set in feudal Japan and introduced the *Total War* series' signature mechanics, a combination of real-time strategy and turn-based empire management.

Shogun was a moderate success, but in 2004, the company released *Rome: Total War* and never looked back.

Rome was set in the Ancient Roman period and featured far improved graphics and excellent gameplay mechanics. *Rome* remains a highly rated game, with its impressive historical accuracy, and even had a stint featuring in a television show. The BBC produced a gameshow called *Time Commanders*, which ran from 2003–2005, and featured gamers competing using a modified version of *Rome: Total War*.

Total War has soared to incredible heights since the early days of *Rome*. Now there are 28 games including expansions, featuring realistic periods such as the Napoleonic Wars, Medieval Europe, the Spartans, and 18th century Empire building. In recent years, Creative Assembly haven't been afraid to push the boundaries, making tie-ins with Warhammer and exaggerated tales of the Three Kingdoms period of Chinese history, taking some inspiration from the *Dynasty Warriors* franchise.

Throughout all iterations, *Total War*'s core system of play has remained consistent. Players manage their empire, in whichever way they please, and use real-time strategy management. The games are known for providing an intense level of difficulty (if you want it to) and are the last word in both historical gaming as well as strategy gaming.

From the early days, Creative Assembly had designs on creating a massive battle scale. In 2000, this was limited, but by the time the franchise had reached *Shogun II* in 2012, the AI could control 56,000 individual soldiers during a single battle. The grand scale of conflict makes the experience cinematic and immersive, whether it's a force of 500 knights facing 10,000 peasants in *Medieval II* or a lone hero battling the almighty *Lu Bu* in one-to-one combat.

The modding community has always excelled in *Total War*, as it does in most PC games. However, one modding community has truly taken the helm in basically creating a brand-new game for the most sought-after franchise of *Lord of the Rings*. Initially, an impressive mod was developed and improved over the 2010s for the *Medieval II* game, but in 2022 a new version was developed for *Rome II* and it's extraordinarily impressive.

Total War players yearn for a true *Lord of the Rings: Total War*, but so far there's no sign of a crossover. Fans continue to wait for any news of what sounds like the ideal combination.

"Look for its coming, at first light of the fifth day. At dawn look to the east…." – Gandalf, *Lord of the Rings: The Two Towers*)

DID YOU KNOW: DWARF FORTRESS

Do you love easy-to-play, accessible gaming that is always fun and never tedious? If you do, then you may find *Dwarf Fortress* disappointing.

Dwarf Fortress is a colony management game that involves establishing an area for your colony of dwarfs that has to survive in a fantastical world. The game was launched in Alpha in 2006 and gamers have sunk thousands of hours into it. *Dwarf Fortress* is all about managing every single aspect of your colony, trying to support the personalities of the colony members and balancing crooked individuals with honest characters that just want to do good.

The game has been compared to *Dungeons and Dragons* for its incredible amount of choice and freedom within the game. It has inspired many other fantasy games like *Minecraft* and *Rimworld,* such is its legacy. Here's a quick look at a few facts about this bizarre game.

1. *Dwarf Fortress* is an early pioneer of *procedurally generated* worlds. This means that the experience is truly unique for

each new playthrough as the world is randomly created and developed as you game. Procedure generation is used in several games nowadays such as *The Binding of Isaac* and *Minecraft*.

2. The graphics of *Dwarf Fortress* are rudimentary and have been since the very start. ASCII art was used as a placeholder by Tarn and Zach Adams, the identical twins who created the game. ASCII is a basic, pixel-y form of animation - the choice was made to help the early software cope with its own limitations. However, it has become a defining feature of the visual style of the experience.

3. From 2006 to 2007, some gamers took part in a Let's Play, which is a recorded playthrough. Given that *Dwarf Fortress* can run a campaign for an exceptionally long time, it should be no surprise that it took almost a year to complete. The campaign has gone down in history as a legendary Let's Play and is known as *Boatmurdered*. There's a ton of written material to go through, should you wish to, with the story containing a mass of catastrophe, epic adventure, and gruesome violence.

4. Historical narrative is at the heart of what makes *Dwarf Fortress* enjoyable. Players can play campaigns that last decades, even hundreds of years, creating a unique and individual history. Each dwarf has their own personality, and a short reign of a barbaric dwarven King can completely alter the next century of dwarf action.

5. There is a series of incredibly well-written stories from *Dwarf Fortress,* which can be found on www.dfstories.com. A

notable example is the *Hamlet of Tyranny*. The story is of unknown origin and follows a fortress built in a region called the hamlet of tyranny. The fortress encountered a supernatural entity called The Entity of Cheese who cursed all the cheese in the fortress. The cheese thus became a malevolent force. As the story develops, the dwarfs who eat the cheese transform into grotesque cheese creatures, leading to a lactose nightmare of a tale that has to be read to be believed.

6. *Dwarf Fortress* currently has no end in sight. Zach and Tarn Adams have both stated that as long as they're alive, they plan on working on *Dwarf Fortress.* Though the game may look like it belongs on a 1981 computer, the style is a testament to its longevity. It's been around for 20 years and the fact that graphics are so rudimentary means that there's no feasible way that it will be *updated* or improved upon. The game only needs to work in ASCII and has features added to it over time. Any game that holds a fanbase after five years is impressive, but 20 years on is astonishing.

7. When you learn a new skill or hobby, most people will refer to it as having "a learning curve." If it's a steep curve, then it means that it will start quite difficult, but eventually get easier as you do it more. Musical instruments are usually described as having a steep curve. *Dwarf Fortress* has a learning *cliff*. In its first iteration, it had no tutorial, and it felt completely impossible. The cluttered menus, difficult…, well, everything and lack of guidance turned a lot of people off within a few minutes. Even with the more recent mountain of knowledge about the game, it takes people a

good few playthroughs at first to understand what they're doing.

Dwarf Fortress has received an update recently and, as of 2022, a graphically improved game is available to buy on Steam, or you can download the original for free. Playing *Dwarf Fortress* is an experience, and not one for everyone, but once you're in, you're *in*. The game is so immersive that you'll struggle to play a game that isn't *Dwarf Fortress* again.

CHAPTER VII: OPEN WORLDS

Before 2010, there weren't tons of open-world games. After 2020, it feels like every game is an open-world game.

Open-world games are games that are set in a world that is..., well, it's open. Players are generally free to explore as they wish, following the main storyline or spending time on other side quests within the game. It became intensely popular, but it was difficult to pull off for many companies. Good open-world games require years of development, and even then, many are left floundering or incomplete on release.

In this chapter, we'll look at the notable open worlds that have helped define the genre. It's worth noting that we've already talked about many open-world games such as *Witcher III, God of War*, and *The SIMS*. There are also more open-world games coming later, so if your favorite open-world isn't mentioned here, it might have already been discussed or you'll find it later in this book.

31. DARK SOULS: OR HOW I LEARNED TO STOP WORRYING AND LOVE DEATH

Trying to enjoy *Dark Souls* is a bit like swallowing toothpicks. It takes longer than you'd think, you'll be in excruciating pain, and you'll wonder why you're bothering to do it.

Dark Souls is the creation of the development studio FromSoftware. The first game, arguably, was *Demon's Souls*, released in 2009. *Demon's Souls* was enjoyable, but the studio fought with Sony for the rights to continue the series, so changed the name to *Dark Souls* and released it in 2011.

Players were intrigued by the gloomy atmosphere at the heart of *Dark Souls* and the mystique around the story. As gamers reach the five-minute mark of the game, they realize the story really isn't important when playing *Dark Souls*. The reason for this is that the game is designed for you to die, over and over and over and over again!

Dark Souls' gameplay is punishing, an almost unbelievably difficult experience. Enemies are uniquely nasty, with skillsets that come out of nowhere if you've not already seen them, and the changing environments are really difficult to manage. But gamers *loved* it. Well, not all gamers, to be fair. Many have played one of the games once and said, "That's too difficult and isn't fun."

FromSoftware has put out three *Dark Souls* games, *Dark Souls II* in 2014 and *III* in 2016, but the franchise really stops there. The company has produced several other games that are in the same vein as *Dark Souls,* with very similar mechanics and aesthetics. *Sekiro* (2019), *Bloodborne* (2015), and *Elden Ring* (2022) are considered to be part of the *Soulsbournes* collective along with *Dark Souls.*

FromSoftware laid a gauntlet down with these games. Gamers can progress through the storyline quickly if they wish, but that makes the experience even more punishing. Players generally spend hours on side quests (which are as difficult as the main story anyway) to build up their stats or collect items. You're allowed to game at your own pace, but it doesn't really matter because you're going to be killed if you run or walk, so do what you like.

The way to enjoy this massive franchise, which boasts more than 33 million sales, is to accept that death is imminent. Even experienced players are caught out by the level design and enemies on offer. Accepting this removes the frustration that can bubble up while playing it, and instead makes it joyful and funny at times. It's hilarious that it's taken you more than 30 attempts to progress past the *same* enemy. It's silly that the boss was down to 1/1000th of its starting health, and it still got you in the end.

Dark Souls isn't for everyone, but it intrigues everyone. The gamers who embark into *this* open world do so knowing what they're getting into, and they love every morsel of it.

32. WOW: THE STANFORD PRISON EXPERIMENT

The Stanford Prison Experiment, conducted in 1971 by psychologist Philip Zimbardo, sought to understand the psychological effects of perceived power and authority. Participants were randomly assigned roles as either prisoners or guards in a simulated prison environment. The study gained notoriety as the "guards" quickly adopted abusive behaviors, leading to its early termination. Surprisingly, a parallel to this experiment unfolded within the virtual world of the popular open-world fantasy online game *World of Warcraft (WoW).*

In 2010, a glitch occurred on one of the *WoW* servers, resulting in players inadvertently being designated as either guards or prisoners, much like in the Stanford Prison Experiment. As players unwittingly assumed these roles, behaviors reminiscent of the original experiment began to emerge. The virtual guards, with their newfound authority, started displaying abusive and authoritarian behaviors toward the prisoners. Reports of virtual harassment, excessive punishment, and dehumanizing treatment circulated within the *WoW* community.

The incident sparked discussions among researchers, gamers, and psychologists about the potential influence of virtual environments on human behavior. It raised questions about the ethical implications of recreating and replicating real-life social experiments within video games, particularly when the lines between fantasy and reality become blurred. While the virtual experiment in *WoW* was a technical glitch rather than a deliberate recreation, it highlights the power of immersive virtual environments to elicit behavioral responses from players. The anonymity provided by online gaming, coupled with the perceived authority granted by assigned roles, can lead to dark or aggressive tendencies in some individuals.

WoW remains a popular game to this day, and most people have heard of it, if not played it at some point. Stories such as the bizarre Stanford Prison Experiment are part of its history, which is now over 15 years in the making.

33. SKYRIM: THE EVERLASTING JAW DROPPER

Bethesda Game Studios tends to just get it right. The company is a specialist in open-world games, managing to dedicate vast sums of money and vast amounts of effort to form memorable worlds that players will explore for a seriously long time. Their catalog boasts three main titles: *Fallout*, *Starfield*, and *Elder Scrolls*.

On November 11, 2011, Bethesda released the fifth *Elder Scrolls* game, *Skyrim*, and this epic open-world RPG would go on to become one of the most enduring and beloved video games in history.

Skyrim is a fantasy open world, very much continuing the work that the previous *Elder Scrolls* games had started. *Elder Scrolls* has always been praised for how much game there is to explore, and for its remarkably detailed environments and side quests. *Skyrim*, however, managed to take this to the next level.

Bethesda packed the game with detail, quests, and bizarre interactions that made *Skyrim* the last word in open-world gaming. *Skyrim* has been so successful that it has been released on three generations of consoles, and someone even managed to program it onto their smart fridge.

It's always impressive when a game outstays its welcome, but *Skyrim* hasn't just outstayed, it's moved into your apartment and started helping itself to your cheese. Its longevity is purely a testament to its infinite replay-ability and impressive lore. The story mode, while exciting on its own, is a tiny portion of the game that, once it's completed, leaves you with tons more to explore should you want the true experience.

If you're a gamer who likes 100%ing games, then you'd have to strap in for a slog. The estimated time for 100%ing *Skyrim* (which includes all objectives and not farting around being silly) is north of 230 hours.

Gamers have been looking for *Elder Scrolls VI* for some time now and - at the time of writing - a trailer has been released. It features gorgeous rolling hills that lead to God only knows what, a fantastical new kingdom or expansion on the incredible lore of the universe? Well, we hope so. Because that's all we got and that was released in 2018. For five years, there's been no decent information to look for and Bethesda seems to be taking their time, for good reason. *Skyrim* was probably the biggest hit of modern gaming (not to mention *Minecraft* and a certain crime open world that we'll discuss later), and the company cannot afford to get it wrong. The long development time for the follow-up to *Skyrim* is a testament to how incredibly important the game is to the fanbase.

34. ANIMAL CROSSING: FORCING HARDCORE GAMERS TO GO "AWW" INVOLUNTARILY

Animal Crossing is a franchise that's been around since 2001, after the first game *Animal Forest* was released on Nintendo 64. This first foray into the gameplay of *Animal Crossing* was an oddly exciting moment, and the series has become a huge success, though it can be confusing to understand why.

Animal Crossing is an open-world game that's about..., doing what you want, really. The game's entire feel is "relaxation" and "calm." Players are offered a virtual world at peace, rather than in the throes of some violent conflict. One plays a character who settles into the neighborhood, helped by their equally cutesy friends, some of whom are anthropomorphized animals.

Players gather collectibles, talk to their friends, build museums, go fishing, play the guitar, really anything that is designed to promote a calming sense of accomplishment. *Animal Crossing* runs a real-time clock and calendar, which forces gamers to come back at different times of the year or try to do certain tasks at night.

The game has been a hit with adults, probably because it allows them a sense of childish escape from the various stresses of adulthood. Or they just like to talk to a talking, walking racoon.

The latest game, *New Horizons,* allowed gamers to take a journey outside of their slightly secluded village, and explore islands, providing chances for discovery and adventure. *New Horizons* was a massive hit because it was released in March 2020. What else was going on then?

Correct, the COVID-19 pandemic. *Animal Crossing* came out at the perfect time as the world was locking down. Adults and children were provided with a calming place to escape to, and to explore while they weren't allowed to continue normal life. *New Horizons* experienced fantastic sales, probably helped by the pandemic, and provided something different.

After all, just look at the rest of the entries in this chapter - how many are about violence or death? Look at the entries of this book! Gamers have a fascination for action when gaming and *Animal Crossing* has done a fantastic job of cornering the market for having a bit of virtual downtime.

35. THE MATRIX ONLINE: RIGHT FORMULA, WRONG EXECUTION

In the early 2000s, a groundbreaking online game emerged that promised to immerse players in the iconic world of *The Matrix* film trilogy. *The Matrix Online,* developed by Monolith Productions and published by Warner Bros. Interactive Entertainment, was a massively multiplayer online role-playing game (MMORPG) released on March 22, 2005. It offered players a unique opportunity to live out their own adventures in the virtual realm of *The Matrix,* but it also became a captivating tale of peculiarities and a legacy that defied expectations.

The Matrix Online offered an innovative and ambitious concept, bridging the gap between movie franchises and online gaming. It aimed to provide players with an evolving storyline, player-driven narratives, and opportunities to interact with well-known characters from *The Matrix* films. Bear in mind that this monumental multiplayer open world was being devised in 2005. *2005!* There was virtually no other studio ready to attempt this monumental task, so it was a serious leap into the abyss for Monolith.

There was good reason for the lack of competition, despite *The Matrix Online*'s intriguing premise and initial success, it faced numerous challenges. The game's servers were shut down on July 31, 2009, just four years after its release, making it one of the shortest-lived MMORPGs of all time. The closure was a disappointment to many fans who had invested time and money in the virtual world.

The reasons for its failure are myriad. Servers were ordered to shut by Warner Bros. as no one seemed to be playing it; in fact, some reports indicated that lows of 500 players were logged on at times. As well as this, the development studio changed halfway through its lifecycle, and lots of cool, live events were just dropped out of nowhere. Not to mention that players were unable to actually fight each other properly because the combat was atrocious.

But really, no one was there to fight. They were there for the community, which showed a bizarrely loving connection between players. By design, the storyline was crafted by the players' actions, a genuinely incredible attempt to craft a story in a new way and it worked…, for a bit. The community would engage in in-game weddings, and large dance parties were held within the Matrix, much to the bewilderment of the developers. When Laurence Fishburne's father died, the community organized an in-game memorial to honor Morpheus, played by Fishburne and to honor his father.

The story of *The Matrix Online* is a strange one. Despite the source material being seen as perfect for video game lore, there's never really been a game that's made it work, though *The Matrix Online* came close and was especially innovative for the mid-

2000s. Its ambitious storytelling approach and community-driven content creation were pioneering concepts that would later influence other online games. Though the servers may have gone dark, the memories of this one-of-a-kind virtual reality experience continue to resonate with those who ventured into the Matrix.

DID YOU KNOW: POKÉMON

Yes, yes, we've spoken about *Pokémon Go* already, but this Did You Know is about *Pokémon* as a franchise.

Pokémon Go may have been the most successful mobile game of all time, but it was built on the back of an almighty empire of open-world gaming that is the *Pokémon* series. *Pokémon,* in most of its forms, puts you in control of a protagonist who goes out into the *Pokémon* world to train up a team of the best Pokémon that they can muster, in order to take out the evil force polluting every inch of the world. It's simple enough in concept, but the execution was always superb (let's not talk about *Pokémon Scarlet & Violet*).

Here are a few Did You Know facts to round off Chapter Seven.

1. In the original *Pokémon* games, there is a glitch known as the "MissingNo" glitch, which allows players to encounter a mysterious glitched *Pokémon* named MissingNo. This glitch is a result of the game's programming and often causes strange graphical distortions. MissingNo could be caught, though possessing it meant it would still fight you and would make

the Hall of Fame feature crash. It's become a bit of a legend of *Pokémon* and it's a great piece to have in your collection.

2. *Pokémon* is no stranger to creating odd creatures for the players to encounter; in fact, it's why the series has lasted so long. The *Pokémon* Drowzee is known to feed on people's dreams. In some Pokedex entries, it is said that a person's dreams can be stolen if they sleep near a Drowzee. In the game "*Pokémon* Platinum," there is a *Pokémon* known as Rotom, which can possess household appliances, turning them into unique *Pokémon* forms, such as Rotom-Wash (washing machine) and Rotom-Heat (oven).

3. In the anime that ties in with the games, there is an episode called "The Legend of Dratini," where Ash and his friends encounter a giant Dratini living in a hidden lake. This episode was banned in several countries due to concerns about showing firearms and violence. These themes aren't typical of *Pokémon,* but they weren't the first nor the last kids show to use firearms to bring a sense of threat. Obviously, they were harshly criticized for their insensitive inclusion in a show aimed at children.

4. As well as the odd *Pokémon* mentioned above (there are many more where that came from), the series isn't afraid to get a bit dark in its lore. Cubone, a quite cute dinosaur-looking *Pokémon* that wears a chalk-white helmet, is a wandering and lost child. Its helmet is no helmet at all, but the skull of its lost mother, which is pretty galling stuff to read. In the *Pokémon* game *Pokémon Black and White,* there is a ghost-type *Pokémon* named Yamask. Its Pokedex entry states that it carries a mask that used to be its human face when it

was alive. The Pokémon may look cute at times, but be careful when reading their origin stories, you might have to sleep with the light on.

5. *Pokémon* are usually used in battle, fighting on their owner's behalf. That's already a weird concept when you consider it. Enslaving unique animals to do battle for you, in most places in the world you'd be put in prison for that. But canonically, Pokémon are animals and some of them are hunted and eaten. The Slowpoke secretes a sweet syrup from its tail, which is eaten as a delicacy in the world of *Pokémon*. It all just gets stranger.

6. Strangely, the people who populate the *Pokémon* games don't seem to bat an eyelid at the frankly astonishing things they've seen. Of course, they live in a world that's inhabited by cute monsters that do battle on an hourly basis, but still, they seem unsurprised by a few amazing events that happen around them. In the world of *Pokémon,* fossils are re-animated and brought back as dinosaur Pokémon, in a scientific feat which is the most incredible display of power ever. Yet Ash and his friends don't care a lot. There are also multiple Pokémon from space. But once again, the humans are nonplussed by the alien Pokémon and confirmation of life outside of their home planet. Perhaps when you've watched your pet yellow squirrel electrocute a giant water dragon, you care less about the world around you.

7. Finally, there's a lot of fun to be had with the Pokémon's names in the game. They're mainly named in Japanese first, which can lead to some humorous mistranslations. The Pokémon Koffing and Weezing, two polluting gas balls,

were originally named Ny and La. As in, "New York" and "Los Angeles," for their overwhelmingly poor pollution in the late 1990s. Zapdos and Jolteon, two electric-type Pokémon also basically have the same name. Zapdos meaning "Thunder," and Jolteon meaning "Thunders."

CHAPTER VIII:
ALL'S FAIR IN WAR AND WAR

Combat features in many games in some fashion, be it a small bout of fisticuffs or a nuclear apocalypse. This chapter deals with the games that are *focused* on armed combat and war.

This is no small genre, there are quite literally thousands of war games that have been created over the last three decades and many of them are fantastic, with plenty that's worth discussing. Some have been naturally disappointing, but that's the gaming industry for you.

In Chapter Eight, we'll deal with some of the biggest titles in war gaming, bringing you strange tales and interesting facts about some of the industry's most beloved shooters.

36. MASTER CHIEF: CREATING AN ICON YOU COULDN'T SEE

Master Chief, the enigmatic protagonist of the *Halo* series, is an exemplary protagonist in the world of first-person shooters. Hidden behind a visor and never seen without his Mjolnir armor, Master Chief is more than just a character - he's an avatar that lets players project themselves into the rich sci-fi universe of *Halo*.

For the uninitiated, the *Halo* games are a science fiction shooter series that follows Master Chief in his battles against the alien Covenant and the parasitic Flood. Starting with *Combat Evolved,* released in 2001, the series provides players with epic first-person campaigns across alien worlds and space stations. *Halo* is respected as one of the greatest video game franchises of all time for good reason, the early online multiplayer was transformative and part of the mid-2000s surge of shooters (along with *CoD*).

Master Chief, known formally as Master Chief Petty Officer John-117, was deliberately designed to be faceless, a decision made by Bungie, the studio that developed *Halo*. This anonymity, much like Link from *The Legend of Zelda,* was aimed at allowing players to easily identify with the character, providing a "blank slate" onto which they could project their own personality and emotions. His Mjolnir armor has become one of the most recognizable and distinctive aspects of the franchise. The armor's design is functional yet intimidating, allowing the players to feel invincible, in much the way that Doomslayer does in the *Doom* franchise.

Master Chief's character and the *Halo Series* draw heavily from various science fiction media. The design of the Mjolnir armor has similarities with the armor seen in *Starship Troopers,* a military science fiction novel by Robert A. Heinlein. Furthermore, the series' expansive universe and story show influences from *Ringworld,* a science fiction novel by Larry Niven.

Master Chief is so recognizable as a character because he's a recognizable protagonist in a shooter game. Franchises try to copy this but very few succeed. *Call of Duty*'s character Soap is often heralded as their attempt to craft a similar experience, but the lack of domineering presence or mystique led that to fall flat. The point is that it's difficult to create a character that grasps a player's attention when they're running out shooting aliens and causing cinematic explosions. *Halo* accomplished it perfectly, with every release bringing a massive amount of attention and money for good reason.

37. THE FALLOUT BOOKS AND THE COLD WAR

Bethesda Game Studio's *Fallout* series has kept players interested in its post-apocalyptic setting and complex stories for decades now. The *Fallout* games, put simply, are an open-world RPG that's set in a world on the receiving end of nuclear war. There's a lot to unpack, but *Fallout* has managed to create a universe around this simple concept, first appearing to gamers in 1997, and creating titles to this day.

The social and political atmosphere of the Cold War is a big part of what makes the game's world what it is. *Fallout* was inspired by this period and considers the fears and worries people had about nuclear war and what would follow. By looking at what would happen after a terrible nuclear war, the series shows how the Cold War changed culture and left a long mark on society.

Fear of a possible nuclear war was a big part of the Cold War, a time of stress and competition between the United States and the Soviet Union. *Fallout* plays on this fear to help draw inspiration for its universe sculpting. In the world of the game, a nuclear war has wiped out most of society, leaving a few people to try to survive in a dangerous, empty wasteland. Taking the worries of the Cold War as a starting point, *Fallout* puts players in a world that has been destroyed by nuclear war.

The *Fallout* series looks at things like government paranoia, progress in technology, and the fight to stay alive in a harsh and unpredictable world. The visuals are heavily inspired by the 1950s and early 1960s, harking back to a bizarre age of consumerism, civil rights issues, and nuclear threat. The game uses "Atomic Age" aesthetics, like retro-futuristic buildings, old ads, Cold War propaganda, and oddly spooky 1940s and 1950s music to put players in a world that reflects the fears and hopes of the time.

In the games, you emerge from a "vault" after a nuclear attack, an underground bunker meant to protect a small number of people from the destruction of a nuclear war. These vaults aren't that far off of what some people built during the Cold War. Some, what would now be called Doomsday preppers, built bomb shelters to safeguard their family in the face of the apocalypse. In *Fallout,* the Vaults are often like miniature versions of society. They show moral problems, power battles, and social experiments that happen when society is in trouble.

The *Fallout* series also looks at the effects of unchecked scientific progress and the possible dangers of advanced technology. In the game's world, there are advanced robots, mutated animals, and scientific groups with unclear morals. These parts serve as warnings, showing how people worried during the Cold War about the moral implications of scientific progress and how it could both help and hurt people.

The franchise has been a monumental success, selling some 46 million copies of its games since 1997, and that number grows weekly. *Fallout 4* shipped a then-record 12 million games at launch, which brought *Bethesda* more than $750 million in one day. Amazon has picked up the rights to make a *Fallout* TV series, which gamers hope is a *Last of Us* success and not an *Assassin's Creed* disaster. If you've never played *Fallout,* then you're seriously missing out. Not every game is a work of art - all fans remember the mess that *Brotherhood of Steel* was - but the universe is undeniably creative.

38. BATTLEFIELD: A LESSON IN FIGHTING CALL OF DUTY AND (SOMETIMES) WINNING

The *Battlefield* franchise was launched in 2002 by *DICE*, beginning with *Battlefield 1942*. This game emphasized large-scale battles, boasting vehicles and destructible environments, both of which weren't always seen in video games. The series has gone on to produce several video games, receiving heavy amounts of praise for its excellent handling of large multiplayer battles. The last notable title, however, came in 2021, which was the now-infamous *Battlefield 2042* - the game was a flop and a real departure in terms of quality.

Battlefield was the subject of one of the great gaming debates of the 21st century: *Call of Duty (CoD)* vs. *Battlefield.*

CoD has grown at almost the same time as *Battlefield*, releasing its first game in 2003. The series focused not on the grand, cinematic scale that Battlefield did, but instead on tighter, fast-paced gameplay and the two series really provided different experiences of war gaming. As time's gone by, *CoD* has done a remarkable job of cornering the market of online shooters and *Battlefield* has never quite competed in terms of raw sales. However, for a while, DICE certainly produced a more consistent product than Infinity Ward & Treyarch.

What *Battlefield* had was innovation, and lots of it. DICE has no pressure to put out a game every year, unlike *CoD*, which gives more time for the development of a new title. When *Battlefield 1* was released in 2016, it blew apart all competition. *1* was a WW1 war simulator, with startlingly grounding physics and graphics that simply left gamers stunned. By contrast, Infinity Ward's competition, *Call of Duty: WWII*, felt flat and uninspiring, just another *CoD* game in comparison to the simulation of *Battlefield 1*.

By the late 2000s, the rivalry was clearly established. Not so much from the companies themselves but from gamers. *CoD*'s releases, *Modern Warfare* and *World at War* were dominant, and it seemed that almost every gamer owned them. DICE wasn't competing until 2011 when they brought out *Battlefield 3* and really showed what their games were about.

Battlefield 3 truly executed large-scale multiplayer. The environments would crumble around the gamer, as explosions tore through cityscapes and scenery. The use of vehicles was miles ahead of *CoD* and the combat was praised for its realism. From *Battlefield 3* in 2011 to *4* in 2013 to *1* in 2016, it felt that DICE was simply making better games than Infinity Ward. The series perfected its signature *Levolution* mechanic to program alterable environments into multiplayer environments to great effect, while expertly jumping from new time period to new time period. *CoD* by comparison felt stuck in the same ideas.

Ultimately, *Battlefield* has never competed with *CoD* on sales figures. *CoD* has managed to sell over 400 million titles over its lifespan, while *Battlefield* hasn't quite reached 100 million. For a while, however, there's a good argument to be had that *Battlefield* made the best online shooters of all time in terms of quality and realism of product.

Ultimately, no one can compete against the behemoth that *CoD* has become, however, as DICE and *Battlefield* players have come to accept.

39. WORMS: CREATING FAMILY FRIENDLY WARFARE

In 1995, a small team of developers known as Team17 unleashed a charming and quirky turn-based strategy game that would captivate players worldwide. *Worms*, the brainchild of Andy Davidson, was released on November 17, 1995, and introduced a delightful blend of strategic gameplay, humorous animations, and absurdly entertaining action. The creation would not only become a gaming phenomenon but also leave a legacy in the realm of family-friendly gaming and violence in video games.

Worms revolutionized the strategy gaming genre through its innovative gameplay mechanics and distinctive art style. It managed to execute some styles of gameplay that we now take for granted. The game allowed players to take control of a team of anthropomorphic worms, each armed with a vast array of zany and destructive weaponry. Fan favorites became the banana bomb, super sheep, and an exploding grandma. It even spawned a popular cult classic called *Hogs of War*, which was largely the same concept but with pigs.

Players took turns planning their moves, aiming shots, and utilizing the terrain to outwit opponents. *Worms* introduced a unique physics engine that simulated environmental destruction, turning the landscape into a chaotic battleground of explosions, collapsing structures, and flying debris.

Worms struck a delicate balance between cartoonish violence and family-friendly fun, which contributed to its impact and appeal. While the game featured weapons and explosions, they were presented in a lighthearted and comedic manner, distancing itself from realistic violence. The turn-based mechanics succeeded in making it accessible to players of all ages, making it an ideal choice for family gaming sessions. The everlasting local co-op multiplayer aspect of *Worms* encouraged friendly competition and cooperation among players, promoting social bonding and communication. If you've ever watched a teenager lose a game of *FIFA*, then you'll understand why this is so important to promote.

Worms spawned an extensive franchise with over 25 sequels and spin-offs, continually evolving its gameplay and incorporating new features while staying true to its core formula. The game became a cultural icon, influencing other titles with its turn-based gameplay and physics-based mechanics. Over the years, *Worms* has found success on various platforms, from PC to consoles, mobile devices, and handheld gaming systems. As *Worms* continues to entertain and unite players worldwide, its unique blend of silliness and strategy has cemented its place in the annals of gaming history as a beloved classic.

40. SPEC OPS: THE LINE—THE WHITE PHOSPHORUS INCIDENT

Spec Ops: The Line, developed by *Yager Development* and released in 2012, is a game that defies expectations and delves into the darker aspects of warfare and human nature. At first glance, it appears to be a standard military shooter, but it takes a dramatic and morally challenging turn during the "White Phosphorus Incident." This shocking moment occurs when the player, controlling Captain Martin Walker, is forced to use white phosphorus munitions on an enemy encampment, only to discover afterwards that the encampment is filled with innocent civilians. The immediate and brutal confrontation of the consequences of players' actions was quite jarring and blurred the lines between heroism and villainy.

In *Spec Ops: The Line*, players follow Captain Walker and his squad as they traverse a post-apocalyptic version of Dubai, devastated by cataclysmic sandstorms. The game's narrative unfolds as a search and rescue mission, with the squad aiming to locate and retrieve a lost U.S. Army colonel, John Konrad, who remained behind to help the survivors.

The White Phosphorus Incident occurs when Walker and his squad come across a heavily defended enemy encampment. Facing overwhelming opposition and believing the enemy to be a significant threat, Walker reluctantly chooses to use white phosphorus munitions as a last resort. The scene is presented with grim intensity, as players unleash a barrage of fiery destruction upon the encampment, thinking they are eliminating enemy combatants.

When the smoke clears, the devastating truth is revealed. The horrific consequences of Walker's actions are revealed, leaving players to grapple with the weight of their choices and the morally gray nature of warfare. The game forces players to confront the harsh realities of war, the fog of conflict, and the difficult decisions soldiers face in chaotic situations.

The controversy surrounding the game was perhaps deserved. Many young gamers get their hands on games that are rated at a far higher age certificate than their age, and young teenagers have to confront the disturbing scene. Many parents thought it was beyond the pale, but the studio remained clear that the point behind including it is more important than the risk of upsetting people.

The incident harked back to a now-famous level from *Call of Duty: Modern Warfare 2*, called *"No Russian,"* which sparked an almighty kickback from media outlets and politicians for its insensitivity. At that level, players are asked to join in with a terrorist act, mowing down thousands of civilians in an airport. Players don't have to join in, but the climate of the world, scarred by extremist-religious terrorism, made it a risky move to include it at all.

Controversies like this are actually quite important. They serve to remind gamers that when they're pretending to be a soldier, springing around the battlefield shooting anonymous NPCs (non-playing characters), they're mimicking a genuinely traumatic and brutal act. *Spec-Ops* managed to pull this off in a manner that was "in your face" but perhaps necessary to remind players just what they're engaging with.

DID YOU KNOW: FORTNITE

If you ask the old guard of gaming "Why is *Fortnite* such a big game?" they will not truly understand why. *Fortnite* has redefined the Battle Royale genre and captured the imaginations of millions since its release on July 25, 2017. Developed by Epic Games, *Fortnite* made its initial debut as a cooperative survival game. However, it was the introduction of its free-to-play Battle Royale mode on September 26, 2017, that catapulted *Fortnite* into unprecedented fame and success.

Fortnite's Battle Royale mode dropped players onto an ever-shrinking island where they fought to be the last one standing. Armed with a pickaxe and the ability to construct structures, players battled not only against each other but also against the encroaching storm that forced them into smaller play areas.

Now a major hit (and by major, we mean almost an estimated $25 billion), *Fortnite* is undeniably a modern warfare classic. In this Did You Know, we'll bring you a few snippets of interesting information and hopefully a small idea of just *how* it became so dominant.

1. *Fortnite* adopted a free-to-play business model, allowing players to download and enjoy the game without any upfront cost. This accessibility was a significant factor in its rapid and widespread adoption. The free-to-play model was previously used by many companies in the 2000s to great success, such as *Runescape* and *Team Fortress* 2. However, there's been a market explosion in free-to-play games since 2017. Why? *Fortnite,* that's why.

2. *Fortnite*'s collaboration with various pop culture franchises, musicians, and artists through in-game events and crossover content made it a digital hub for pop culture. We can discuss things like innovative game design and mechanics all day, but ultimately some people just like to see Thanos from *Avengers* in the game. Those integrations have kept *Fortnite* an outrageously successful franchise.

3. The game of *Fortnite* initially had nothing to do with the Battle Royale mode that has catapulted it into the stratosphere of bestselling games. It was a co-op survival game, where players had to live for two weeks (hence it being called *Fortnite*), fighting off hordes of zombies from their fort. The Battle Royale mode was adopted after the studio saw *PUBG* popularize the mode, and they decided to add it in as a Beta to see if gamers would like it. They did.

4. Epic Games, the company that made *Fortnite,* changed their entire game plan because of Fortnite. For a long time, the studio had been advertising and pushing a title called *Paragon,* which was essentially their favorite child. *Paragon* had its fans, but Epic Games decided to put all its eggs into one basket. Not a bad basket to choose!

5. Though the series popularized free-to-play, it wasn't always that way. In fact, in the very early days of its release in 2017, you had to buy a disk edition to play it. If you happen to have the original disk edition, it can be sold for an overwhelming amount of money (especially considering it's literally free!).
6. For the old gamers or the old parents of gamers, reading, this may seem a bit of a foreign idea. But by using websites such as *Fiverr*, players can hire a coach to help them get better at Fortnite. These coaches, the good ones, charge $35–40 per hour to assist you in..., not dying. The *Wall Street Journal* published an article on this a couple of years ago, shocking parents that their little darlings might be paying hundreds of dollars for this form of private education.
7. In 2019, Epic started proceedings to sue a 14-year-old boy. Yes, you read that right. The teenager was selling ways for how to cheat at *Fortnite* online and making some money from it. He was giving software to people that he hadn't created to help them cheat, and *Fortnite* is claiming damages for loss of earnings. He's not the only one in the suit, and he faces a $150,000 fine if he's found guilty.

CHAPTER IX: CRIMINALLY GOOD GAMING

Crime doesn't pay, but it does pay if you make a game about it.

Why is crime such a good genre for gaming? Perhaps it's because most of us wouldn't ever pursue a life of being "bad," but to do so on a video game allows us to try the darker side of life. Or maybe because many games about crime are well crafted and we like them.

In this chapter, we'll look at a few games focused on the criminal world, and we promise that it's not just going to be a *Rockstar* chapter.

41. HITMAN: IT DOESN'T MATTER HOW, JUST DO IT

The *Hitman* franchise gets our crime world gaming started. *Hitman* is one of those games that seems to have been around forever, with Eidos Interactive producing *Hitman: Codename 47* in 2000. The player controls Agent 47, a ruthless assassin for hire, who takes part in a series of levels aimed at taking out a target. As the games have evolved, the possibilities and freedom afforded have only increased, and you can be surprisingly inventive in more modern games. There's something freakishly exhilarating about walking out of the level with pandemonium escalating around you, as people wonder how on earth the President's son could have accidentally choked to death on a banana.

Hitman promotes exploration through its clever and obliquely humorous Easter eggs, and there's a variety to feast on.

In *Hitman 2*, Agent 47 attends a party at a villa owned by a Russian general. After some exploring, the agent discovers the general's hidden torture chamber, which has a slight undertone of sexuality that baffled gamers in 2002. In 2012, *Hitman: Absolution* hit consoles and players were delighted to find that you could assassinate someone with laxatives. Spiking the victim led to a humorous and slightly gross demise but trademarked how well the franchise sneaks humor into a serious subject.

The series is praised for what is known as the "Creative Kill System," which has been in play since 2004's *Hitman: Contracts.* Early on, developers saw that the way to make Hitman a fun crime thriller and not just a stealth game (or even worse a shoot 'em up) was to give freedom to the players.

Since 2004, the amount of creativity and freedom that is worked into each level is genuinely impressive. Players can make deaths look like accidents, or they can choose to frame someone if they so wish, so long as the outcome is the same. The programming behind *Hitman* is very impressive and not easily pulled off.

Agent 47 is a bit of a legend in the world of gaming. An unemotional, uncaring machine that never seems phased by anything, it's a great character to take control of. It also allows the developers to focus purely on the whole "assassinating" aspect of the game and not to get bogged down in character development. The players do not want Agent 47 to be developed.

42. HEAVY RAIN: BETTER STORYTELLING THAN THE SOPRANOS!

(WARNING, SPOILERS AHEAD!)

Heavy Rain, developed by Quantic Dream and released in 2010, is a gripping interactive drama that captivated players with its intricate storyline and emphasis on player choices. The game follows the lives of four protagonists, each connected to the case of the mysterious Origami Killer, who kidnaps young boys and drowns them in rainwater.

Throughout *Heavy Rain*, players control Scott Shelby, a private investigator hired by the families of the Origami Killer's victims to find the culprit. As players guide Shelby through his investigations, they witness his tenacity, compassion, and apparent commitment to bringing the killer to justice. The game expertly employs red herrings and misdirection, leading players to believe that Shelby is a force for good, fighting to uncover the truth behind the gruesome murders.

However, as the game progresses and the stories of the other protagonists unfold, subtle clues and hints begin to surface, suggesting that Shelby may not be who he appears to be. The game skillfully plants some seeds of doubt, encouraging players to question Shelby's motives and actions. As the various storylines converge, the truth about Shelby's identity gradually unravels, culminating in a shocking reveal.... He *is* the Origami Killer!

The moment when Scott Shelby is unmasked as the Origami Killer is a true surprise that upends players' expectations. The revelation challenges their assumptions and forces them to reevaluate the character they have controlled throughout the game. It is a testament to *Heavy Rain*'s narrative craftsmanship, creating a sense of tension and suspense while delivering a shocking twist that has a profound impact on the story's outcome.

The significance of this twist extends beyond the initial shock value. It raises thought-provoking questions about the nature of good and evil, the capacity for deception, and the depths of human darkness. The twist shows blurred lines between heroism and villainy, which is especially important in a crime game. Games often make us see the world in a binary fashion, *Heavy Rain* showed us that it never is that way.

Heavy Rain brought a game about crime to a different level and gave it depth. There was no ham-fisted attempt to add some deeper level of meaning, it was simply great writing that revealed the story slowly. Fans have called for a sequel, but there doesn't seem to be anything on the horizon, upsettingly.

43. GRAND THEFT AUTO: MAKING PARENTS VERY, VERY UPSET FOR 25 YEARS

You thought that we'd left it out in the open-world chapter, didn't you? Admit it! Of course, we hadn't forgotten about *Grand Theft Auto,* one of the most famous franchises ever created and without a doubt the most controversial one.

The *Grand Theft Auto* (*GTA*) series, made by Rockstar Games, has become known for its huge open-world settings and immersive gameplay. One of the things that makes the series stand out is how well it recreates real towns, capturing the spirit and atmosphere of famous places. From *Liberty City,* which was based on New York City, to *Vice City,* which was based on Miami, to Los Santos, which was based on Los Angeles, the *GTA* series shows how hard the game designers worked to study and recreate these cities.

GTA lets players explore huge, open-world environments that have that *feel* of a real place. Admittedly the early games struggled to capture this. Earlier titles such as *Grand Theft Auto II* and the early *Grand Theft Auto London* expansion (which gamers have cried for a re-make or sequel for) employed a top-down perspective. To be fair, the perspective fails to render much sense of realism, but what else were they supposed to do in 1997?

GTA is frankly an outrageous game that offers a stunning amount of free choice to gamers. The games are often seen as playgrounds, rather than a restrictive series of levels. There is a story mode of course, but it's up to the gamer if they'd like to follow that. Many would happily admit that the best times aren't completing the carefully thought-out levels but speeding around in a sports car with the entire city's police force and army out to get you. The best moments were when, in *San Andreas*, a tank would be brought out to stop you..., of course, you'd just steal the tank and become indestructible!

Rockstar has never been afraid to have fun with *GTA*. They stuff the games with silly Easter eggs, hidden secrets, and cheats to just let the players enjoy themselves. The cheats are things of legend. Back in the days of *San Andreas*, there were cheats for just about anything you wanted. You could remove your wanted level, you could increase your wanted level to full, you could make all NPCs aggressive, you could make boats fly, or just spawn yourself a jet plane.

Though the series has been huge ever since it was created, arguably its latest installment has been the most groundbreaking. *Grand Theft Auto V* was released in 2013, though you wouldn't know that. *GTA V* is still played every day by literally millions of people.

The game has been remastered for each new generation of console, which has helped, but it's mainly been down to the

Online mode. *GTA Online* has created a world of possibilities, goals, achievements, and all sorts of things that players have sunk their teeth (and wallets) into. Few games last a decade and even fewer have their online portion last that length of time.

GTA is also helped by its reputation. In a world where you can do anything, you can do *anything*. Gamers go on murderous rampages, steal expensive cars, cause major pileups, engage in illegal drugs, gamble, and just about everything illegal. It's caused its fair share of controversy with some cautious parents concerned about the effect it has on the developing mind.

There's no denying it. *GTA* is one of the dominating game series, which helps to legitimize the gaming industry as a serious force compared to other entertainment industries. *GTAV* has so far made almost $8 billion on its own. No movie has ever come close to that level of financial success, and it's undeniably impressive.

44. DRIVER: THE MOST DIFFICULT MINUTE OF GAMING EVER?

- Burnout
- Handbrake
- Slalom
- 180°
- 360°
- Reverse 180°
- Speed
- Brake Test
- Lap

If you recognize this list, then you know true pain.

For the uninitiated, that is the list of driving techniques that you must show in the tutorial level of the 1999 PlayStation 1 classic *DRIVER*. You are given a generous 60 seconds to show off your skills in an underground car park with a passenger who is none too impressed by your ability.

DRIVER is a game where you drive. You play as a former racecar driver turned detective, tasked with engaging criminals in car chases and bringing them to justice, in homage to various 1970s action movies. *DRIVER* features an open world and the ability to drive around it as you please, exploring the city, with a lucky ability to engage in some light crime. Well, whatever crime you can get up to while inside your car, that is because, in the first two games, players weren't able to leave their vehicle.

You may be thinking, "This is all well and good, but why have I been told about the tutorial before anything else?" The reason is that the *DRIVER* tutorial is the only bit of the game that many gamers ever got to see. It's the very first level and is outrageously difficult, more difficult than any other part of the game by far.

The controls were pretty good for a 1999 game, but even so, the short list of precise skills, which sometimes weren't recognized by the game even when you'd definitely done them, was painful.

DRIVER was a hit though. In 1999, it pulled off an incredible open world, with some fantastic missions that were genuinely exhilarating. Failure was easy if you drove poorly, and that's what it was about: Hunting down the crime families of the world as the driver.

The series unfortunately peaked with *DRIVER*. After a point, *GTA* did the driving better than *DRIVER* did when it went to a 3D environment, meaning there wasn't much point to playing it anymore. The series has continued, putting out a game here and there, but it's failed to dominate gaming in more recent years.

What *DRIVER* is remembered for, however, is creating great reworks of real-world cities Miami, San Francisco, Los Angeles, and New York City and nailing driving mechanics while it was at it. Many argue that *DRIVER* gave a reason for Rockstar to adopt the 3D style of gaming, abandoning the tired top-down aesthetic, and to start really pushing the boat out in the 2000s.

It'll also be remembered for being so difficult that more than half the players were never able to get past the tutorial.

45. PAYDAY: THAT OPENER FROM DARK KNIGHT IS REALLY GOOD, ISN'T IT?

In 2008, Christopher Nolan released arguably the best superhero film of all time, *The Dark Knight*, which is about Batman and his battle with the Joker. For all of the film's amazing moments, amazing dialogue, and character development, many people became obsessed with the first seven minutes.

In the first part of the movie, an intricate bank heist plays out, whereby the Joker masterminds the capture of millions of dollars, executing his accomplices in a pretty amazing scene. The robbers all wore exaggerated clown masks during the heist, which undeniably had an impact on the aesthetic of *Payday*, which graced the gaming world in 2011.

Payday is a simple game series in principle, developed by Overkill Software. Players assume the role of criminals executing heists on different buildings.

The game is best enjoyed co-operatively, with many gamers loving the engaging necessity to play with friends or try to work with strangers. It was a brave move; in 2011, the landscape of gaming was very much moving to individual glory in online gaming. Sports games like *FIFA* were kicking off their online modes, while *Call of Duty*, *Battlefield*, and *World of Warcraft* were raking in massive cash for their online modes.

The first game was a success, however, and Overkill quickly moved to producing *Payday 2*, which went on to have astronomical success. The sequel managed to sell around 20 million copies across PlayStation, XBOX, and PC, with its popularity not seeming to have an end.

Payday sometimes bases itself on real-life heists, taking inspiration from the North Hollywood shootout and other hostage situations. An air of legitimacy and genuine tension is added to the mix by the expertly crafted score from Simon Viklund, who perfectly places you in the atmosphere of a criminal gang out to make their millions.

The series is a huge hit and is set to release its third iteration. Expect more of the same, with some huge innovations as technology, has improved greatly over the last decade. What is for sure is that the dedicated fan base will purchase it in their thousands, if the current success of the series is anything to go by.

DID YOU KNOW: BULLY: CANIS CANEM EDIT

Being totally fair, this game isn't explicitly about *crime* per se, but it does feature criminal acts and being a bit bad—which is good enough for us!

If you weren't gaming in 2006, then you'll have missed the now infamous *Bully: Canis Canem Edit,* which was released by Rockstar for the PlayStation 2. The game plays similarly to *GTA,* it's a third-person perspective, open-world, action-adventure style game. Set in the town of Bullworth, players control Jimmy, who is put into a boarding school in order to rise through the ranks of the school to put a stop to bullying.

What every player did, however, was just bully every other pupil in ways that would test even the most patient of teachers. Parents and teachers despised the game, but it was hilarious fun for every school-age gamer who'd inappropriately gotten hold of a copy.

Here's a Did You Know about *Bully: Canis Canem Edit,* and some interesting tidbits about Jimmy and Bullworth.

1. The game is not really called *Bully: Canis Canem Edit*. It was simply called *Bully* in its American release, but in Europe and Australia, this was seen as to condone bullying. So, in those regions, it was simply *Canis Canem Edit*, which means *Dog Eat Dog* in Latin.
2. Much like the high schools of the mid-2000s, the school was divided into factions or "cliques" including Nerds, Bullies, Preppies, Greasers, Jocks, and Townies. It's up to the player how you interact with these cliques. They each have their own personalities and characteristics, and your interactions will change the play of the game. So, think carefully before you give the Nerd a wedgie; you may just need them later on.
3. There are a few Easter eggs regarding *Bully*. There are near-constant references to other Rockstar games like *GTA* and *Manhunt*, insinuating in some fashion that the Rockstar universe is connected somehow. Hilariously, Jimmy might also feature in *Grand Theft Auto V*, pretending to be Sasquatch in the forest, though that is unconfirmed. Bullworth Academy is shown in *GTAIV* in an episode of *I'm Rich*.
4. The game has been praised for the interactions that can take place between the NPC characters, which help bring Bullworth Academy to life. If Jimmy kisses someone in front of his former partner, then they'll actually start fighting over Jimmy. Should another NPC come over to watch, they can be heard telling Jimmy to "sit back and relax."
5. Bully was a topic of serious debate at its release. In Florida, a concerned activist tried to get the game banned due to its

depiction of violence in schools, but the presiding judge simply responded - "It's no worse than you see on TV every night." In the UK, the Film Classification Board refused to rate it, and there were concerns that it wouldn't be permitted for release there at all. This isn't the first time Rockstar has run into problems. *GTA* has faced significant controversy and *Manhunt* was actually banned across Europe for several years.

6. The initial design for *Bully* was set to be incredibly dull. Rockstar was looking into making a "boarding school simulator," as if kids want to come home from school to then..., go to school. Eventually, someone must have said, "No, that sounds terrible," and the game morphed into what we see today.

7. *Bully* received criticism for its depiction of teenage romance, and has ever since. Jimmy can conduct romantic relationships, but there's nothing too explicit in there, especially as *Rockstar* wanted to keep the *Teen* rating. But that didn't stop concerned parents from campaigning against the release and the potential sexualizing of school kids. It never gained enough traction to prevent the game's release, but it's been a strange point of contention ever since, especially considering that Jimmy is only 15 himself in the game.

CHAPTER X: JOURNEYING THROUGH TIME

Unfortunately, this is the last chapter, *Journeying Through Time*.

This last chapter is an examination of some notable games that looked back into history for their settings or even looked forward to imagining a future world. All games are, of course, set in "a time," but these games incorporate the historical element with unmatched expertise.

Enjoy the last chapter, then we'll meet again at the end for a goodbye.

46. RED DEAD REDEMPTION: BRINGING CLINT EASTWOOD TO YOUR CONSOLE

(SPOILERS AHEAD!)

In the vast and immersive open world of *Red Dead Redemption*, players embark on a gripping journey through the dying days of the Wild West, at the end of the 19th century. Developed by Rockstar Games and released in 2010, the game masterfully blended storytelling, action, and exploration, captivating players with its richly detailed world and compelling characters. The series was only improved by *Red Dead Redemption 2*, which was a stunning visualization of a grand, epic Western movie with enough content to keep you busy until you retire.

In the first game, you play as John Marston, a former outlaw seeking redemption and a peaceful life for his family. Marston navigates the vast landscapes of the southern United States, engaging in thrilling gunfights, and making morally complex choices that shape the narrative. As players progressed through the game, they witnessed Marston's growth, his struggles, and his unwavering determination to leave his violent past behind.

John Marston's death was a pivotal and heart-wrenching turning point in the game's narrative and undeniably contributed to the game leaving such a mark on modern gaming. After a long and arduous journey to secure a pardon from the government, Marston finds himself betrayed and hunted by the very agents he thought he could trust. In a desperate last stand, he valiantly defends his family, but ultimately succumbs to a hail of bullets, sacrificing himself to ensure their safety.

Marston's death serves as a narrative catalyst, propelling the story forward and providing a thematic exploration of the cycles of violence and the inescapable nature of the Wild West era. The player is abruptly thrust into the role of Marston's son, Jack, who must carry on his father's legacy and seek justice for his untimely death. This transition creates a sense of continuity while also highlighting the cyclical nature of violence.

Across the whole backdrop, there's this sense that Marston's old way of life is dying out. The days of gunslinging cowboys are being left behind at the turn of the century. America truly looks like a changing world, with modernity creeping in, even in remote towns that wish to be left alone. Throughout it all, the locomotive snakes through the landscape, belching black smoke into the air, reminding the player that these days of horses and carts are about to end.

The second game, which was called *Rootin' Tootin' Cowboy Shootin'* (only joking, it was called *Red Dead Redemption 2),* brought the game back in time and John Marston is a side character instead of the protagonist. *RDR2* has entered the conversation of "best game of all time" and it's certainly impressive. The Wild West is better realized than in the first game and the world is incomprehensibly vast and detailed.

However, it was truly the first *Red Dead Redemption* that had more to say about the history of America. Pointing forward and creating a commentary that was quite a bit more than "Grand Theft Auto on horses."

Also, it had a zombie expansion game that was fantastic.

47. GHOST OF TSUSHIMA: A DANCE BETWEEN HISTORY AND FICTION

Sucker Punch Productions, a studio renowned for its work on the *Infamous* series, took a bold step in the opposite direction of superheroes and urban landscapes with its next project. The result was *Ghost of Tsushima,* an action-adventure game set in 13th-century Japan. The narrative centers around Jin Sakai, a samurai warrior whose life takes a dramatic turn during the Mongol invasion of Tsushima Island. He adapts to unconventional warfare to become "The Ghost" and leads an effective resistance against the Mongol forces. This move was risky. This is a historical context that most Western audiences are quite ignorant of, so the studio really rolled the dice on this.

Yet the history is just one part of what the game represents, with a mass of trivia, historical context, and cultural nuances lying beneath. The game became a huge hit, selling close to ten million copies since it was released in 2020. It managed to highlight a period of history often ignored by the media and brought some attention to Japanese culture as well.

Jin Sakai's journey is about conflict, both external and internal. On one hand, he battles the Mongols; on the other, he grapples with the rigidity of his samurai code. His journey expertly showed the historical tension between the samurai's adherence to Bushido and the necessity of subterfuge and espionage in warfare, practices that would later be associated with ninjas.

A significant source of inspiration for *Ghost of Tsushima* was the work of legendary filmmaker Akira Kurosawa. The game's Kurosawa Mode, which turns the visuals into black-and-white and adds film grain, is a homage to the director's signature style. Sucker Punch even sought and received approval from Kurosawa's estate to use his name for this mode.

While *Ghost of Tsushima* draws heavily from historical events, it's not a historical simulator. Sucker Punch took creative liberties to craft a story that's both engaging and respectful of the source culture. For instance, the Mongol invasion depicted in the game happened in 1274, but the katana, Jin's primary weapon, didn't come into use until a few centuries later. This choice was made to align with the popular perception of samurais wielding katanas.

Ghost of Tsushima's open world isn't just a battleground; it's a character in its own right, guiding players in subtle ways. Sucker Punch eschewed traditional navigational UI for a more immersive mechanic - the "Guiding Wind." This mechanic uses the game's wind to guide players to their objectives, a tribute to the significance of nature in Japanese culture.

The game's unique sound design enhances its authenticity. The flute melodies played by Jin were created using a Shakuhachi, a traditional Japanese flute. Similarly, the Tsugaru Jamisen, another traditional Japanese instrument, was used for the background score during stealth sequences.

For players seeking an immersive experience, the game offers a Japanese language option with English subtitles. However, Sucker Punch added a touch of authenticity here too. The subtitles aren't a direct translation of the Japanese dialogues but are adapted to capture the spirit of the conversation, highlighting the studio's respect for cultural nuances.

In the midst of combat and chaos, *Ghost of Tsushima* provides serene moments where Jin composes Haiku, a form of Japanese poetry. This gameplay mechanic is not just a cultural nod but also a reflection of Jin's personality, reinforcing the duality of his character - a ruthless warrior and a sensitive soul.

Ghost of Tsushima is a fusion of cultural reverence, historical touchstones, and creative storytelling. Its meticulously crafted world, coupled with intricate gameplay mechanics and a deeply personal narrative, offers an experience that is genuinely different from what is usually served up by major game studios. Its historical context may be difficult to grasp for Western audiences, but it's thrilling and brazenly original.

48. CRUSADER KINGS: TAKING HISTORICAL ACCURACY TO AN ALMOST BORING POINT

Earlier in the book, we discussed the *Total War* series. That is an empire management game with a focus on diplomacy and in-battle strategy. Often mentioned in the same breath is the *Crusader Kings* series, an empire management game with a focus on diplomacy and strategy. The difference is the in-battle strategy, which isn't a feature of the *Crusader Kings* games.

Crusader Kings is all about forging a Medieval dynasty over centuries. Where *Total War* is a bit light on intricate diplomacy, *Crusader Kings* gives the player a remarkable amount of control over it. Gamers are in charge of the kingdom's economic, military, and political success while managing organized religion, stability, and familial relationships with other dynastic powers.

Some gamers have criticized *Crusader Kings* for being just a *touch* dull. The drama is in the role-playing elements, cemented in a defined period.

The Medieval era attracted considerable interest from modern audiences. People think of Henry VIII, civil wars, month-long sieges, princesses, vast empires, and constant conflict. There are innumerable TV shows and movies set in this era, so it's no surprise that *Crusader Kings* has its audience.

As a series, *Crusader Kings* is unapologetically complex. Paradox, who make the series, has never toned down the involved nature of the engine, not even for console gamers (who are often given less complex versions of games - patronizing, of course, but deserved). When there's an engine as perfected and complex as this, however, it's a master for storytelling, and gamers love to share their individual tales of woe and success.

Reddit user Mackntish wrote a dramatic retelling of their time on *Crusader Kings III*, in which their husbands kept dying. Four Kings were slain in eight years and the disruption caused major revolts across the empire, as civilians were uneasy about the constant death. After 20 in-game years, the truth finally emerged. It was the central character's twin all along! Through the spectacularly designed random element, the game had created an evil, vindictive twin with a murderous obsession.

If Medieval history and role-playing are up your street, then *Crusader Kings* is for you. Mind you, if Medieval history and role-playing are things you already enjoy, you probably already own the game.

49. HORIZON ZERO DAWN: A JURASSIC FUTURE

Horizon Zero Dawn, a post-apocalyptic game set in a world populated by majestic, robotic dinosaurs, was developed by Dutch video game developer Guerilla Games, known for the *Killzone* series. It is an action role-playing game that places players in the role of a character named Aloy, a brave and skilled huntress on a mission to uncover her origins and the truth of the world she inhabits.

The main story unfolds in the 31st century, in a world where humanity is no longer the dominating species, replaced by often aggressive robotic creatures known colloquially as "machines." The game portrays a dichotomy of high-tech artificial intelligence juxtaposed against tribal societies of humanity, creating a world that seems 80,000 years in the past, yet 1,000 years in the future. Traversing this diverse landscape, Aloy uncovers the truth about her own origin, the history of the Old World, and the events that led to its downfall.

The developers at Guerilla Games spent over five years crafting *Horizon Zero Dawn.* The idea of the game was one among 40 proposals that the development team considered after finishing

Killzone 3. They were aiming for a novel concept, a drastic departure from their typical FPS genre. This daring venture into uncharted territory spawned *Horizon Zero Dawn*, a game whose unique premise would captivate players worldwide.

Aloy, the name of the protagonist, sounds similar to "alloy," a metal made by combining two elements. This not only symbolizes her connection with the machines but also her dual nature as a bridge between the old and the new world. The studio was praised heavily for bringing an original, cool, and unsexualized female lead to a major video game franchise. She's a role model, often pitched as a more modern, futuristic Lara Croft.

The world of *Horizon Zero Dawn* is rooted in Earth's familiar landscapes, subtly altered by the passage of time and the reign of machines. This was accomplished through a delicate fusion of known and foreign elements, designed to create a sense of uncanny familiarity. The game's world draws inspiration from locations such as Colorado, Utah, and parts of Nevada for the main map. The Frozen Wilds expansion further added Yellowstone National Park to this list.

An incredible amount of detail went into the machines' design. The developers studied countless hours of wildlife footage to mimic real-life animal behavior accurately. Furthermore, the designs were inspired by real dinosaurs and modern machines. One example is the machine "Thunderjaw," which resembles a Tyrannosaurus Rex combined with heavy artillery weaponry, to create an entirely new, yet familiar, creature. This tone of familiar yet brand new is consistent throughout the games, and it's utterly unique.

A central part of *Horizon Zero Dawn* is its tribal cultures, each with its distinct customs and beliefs. These tribes are not merely imaginative creations but are intricately designed with influences from real-world cultures. The Nora tribe, to which Aloy belongs, shows inspiration from Native American cultures. The Carja, on the other hand, display a mix of influences, primarily Mayan and Ancient Egyptian cultures, apparent in their sun-worshipping religion, architecture, and tendency to build large structures. Set 1,000 years in the future, with humanity's empire destroyed, the game explores the interesting question of what survives. Perhaps it is the old ways and traditions of the ancient civilizations that will outlast the technological achievements of our worshipped tech-gods: Zuckerberg, Jobs, and Musk.

The glyphs seen in the game have a story of their own. The developers collaborated with a historical linguist to create a unique pictographic script for the Carja tribe, inspired by ancient Chinese, Egyptian, and Mayan hieroglyphs. Each pictograph correlates to a word or phrase, enabling the game to tell stories through visual cues.

While *Horizon Zero Dawn*'s story of a post-apocalyptic Earth is central to its appeal, the intricate, meticulously constructed world brimming with hidden details and thoughtful nuances truly sets it apart. The trivia and fascinating facts about its creation make the game an even more awe-inspiring experience. Bizarrely, the games haven't quite succeeded as much as may have been expected. *Zero Dawn* and *Forbidden West* have together sold 32 million copies, which is impressive, but *Horizon* has been a flagship for Sony for about five years. Perhaps its unique viewpoint and philosophical elements have prevented the game from topping the sales charts, where the more familiar titles tend to reign supreme.

50. TIMESPLITTERS: THE SEQUEL MUST BE COMING ANY DAY NOW...

If you like being able to turn off whatever video game you are playing and continue your normal life with functioning vision, then you'll hate *TimeSplitters*.

TimeSplitters is an FPS series released between 2000 and 2005, though there may be more to come (more on this in a bit). *TimeSplitters* had a unique ability to combine fast-paced gameplay, AI-controlled characters in multiplayer mode, and bright flashy visuals, causing players to see dancing spots in their eyes for up to ten days after their gaming session.

TimeSplitters is a bit of a lost relic in gaming history. Three games were produced within five years and were spectacular successes, for the time. Taking elements from successful shooters like *GoldenEye,* they managed to make a well-functioning and simple-to-play FPS game. Where they differed from most, especially in 2005, was in their decision to mess about with time travel.

TimeSplitters focuses on Sergeant Cortez, the series' protagonist, as he journeys back and for in time as part of the Space Marine force whose job it is to take down the TimeSplitters. The TimeSplitters are an alien race that travels through time, dimensions, and space as part of a 500-year-long war against humanity. The result of the introduction of time travel to the past and the future is a really engaging story, plus varied-level design, which can be hard to come by in FPSs from the mid-2000s. Most prominent, however, is the frankly bizarre sense of humor on display.

The creators, Free Radical Design, had a lot of fun with the series. They used a massive amount of pop culture references, let you play as silly characters, and allowed the game to not take itself seriously at all. You could control a remote cat, play as a dissected cow carcass, battle zombie moose, mess around with experiments, zap ghosts, and fight a monkey…and that's only in one game. *TimeSplitters* gained a serious following of gamers and then, after the release of *Future Perfect* in 2005, the game blinked out of existence.

Free Radical Design initially announced that there would be another *TimeSplitters* game on the horizon, and fans wouldn't have to wait long. But that didn't come to fruition.

The company collapsed after helping to create the often forgotten and hated game *Haze*, and *TimeSplitters 4* seeped into the background. In 2012, the developers announced that there would be no further *TimeSplitters* games and that they feared there was no fanbase left for the uniquely odd series. In response to this, a fan group emerged that announced they would create a new *TimeSplitters* game called *Rewind* that would allow players to play a version of the games online on PC.

Since then, the fan game has been in slow development and a few hundred thousand gamers have awaited irregular updates for the last decade. Now, in 2023, it seems like some progress is being made, and the game isn't far from being released for free - good news for TimeSplitters fans! Since then, Free Radical Design has reformed and announced that the eponymous *TimeSplitters 4* is now in development and is on the way soon.

It's a race against time for the fans and for the developers. By the time any products are released, will they be able to capitalize on a new generation of gamers? Or will they be stuck with the dwindling old guard, who are themselves beginning to time travel into a future that involves more kids of their own and less garish, flashy, time-warping, shooters?

DID YOU KNOW: METAL GEAR SOLID

Did you seriously think that we'd leave this out? One cannot make a book based on video game trivia and notable games across our history without mentioning one of the world's most bizarre series of them all: *Metal Gear Solid*.

Metal Gear is a series of stealth-action video games made by Konami and designed by Hideo Kojima. The first *Metal Gear* game came out in 1998, and since then, the series has become known for its complicated stories, dark humor, and new ways to play.

The story of the game series is about Solid Snake, a famous soldier and spy who fights against different bad guys and military threats, mainly set in a warped version of the 20th century. The series takes a few (and by "a few" we mean "a lot of") leaps of imagination and moments of creative license to teach us a bit about the tensions surrounding the Cold War.

Unfortunately, *Metal Gear Solid* seems to be in limbo. Hideo Kojima, the visionary behind the games, left Konami in 2015. Since then, Konami made one more title, *Metal Gear Survive,* which may genuinely be one of the worst games ever. There are remasters and such on the way, but the future of the series remains uncertain.

Regardless, there's lots to unpack here. This Did You Know may seem a bit strange for people who haven't heard of the series before. If you've played it though, then you know just how weird it can be, so will be prepared for anything.

1. In the fantastic third game *Snake Eater*, Solid Snake fights a unique fight against a veteran sniper. The gamer is tasked with finding the old man who is hidden in the thick jungle. It's a tense battle, and you never know when you'll be shot by the wizened soldier, but in a hilariously innovative fashion, you don't have to fight him at all. If you simply wait, then he dies of old age, and you can pass on without any trouble or expenditure of bullets at all!

2. In *Metal Gear Solid*, released in 1998, the developers used incredible ingenuity in creating the villain Psycho Mantis. Many gamers are already aware of his powers, but in the battle, the boss reads your memory card, takes over your controller, and seems to change the channel on the TV. The moment is actually quite freaky, and many gamers were left baffled when they first encountered him.

3. In *Snake Eater*, on the PS2 version (and only this one), players can access a secret mini game called *Guy Savage*. You play as Big Boss has a nightmare about a man fighting off many zombies in a frankly superb mini game. The controls are completely separate from *Snake Eater*, and the whole thing is irrelevant to the experience of the game. Guy Savage was envisioned as its own

full game in the future, but it wasn't to be. The dream sequence was a way of putting a sneaky demo out into the world.

4. *Metal Gear Solid 4* was created as an act of protest. The game features an aged Snake and a spectacularly out-there plot line, even for Kojima. The story goes that the visionary developer wanted out of the *Metal Gear* project, but Konami nailed him down to continue creating games for the successful series. Kojima decided that if he had to do it, then he'd do whatever the hell he wanted with it, and it's all the better for his decision to do so.

5. *Metal Gear Solid 2* may not have happened at all. In the second game, you play as Solid Snake, then later you play as Raiden, accomplishing missions in the same location that Snake was in. When you're Raiden, everything you do is eerily similar to how it was in the first half of the game and many fans were questioning what the point of it was. After a while, you end up in a dreamscape-like world where all of your clothes are removed, and nothing makes any sense at all. Fans have theorized that none of it actually happens, only existing in a virtual-reality-like world. With Kojima, you can't count anything out.

6. For the 1998 title, Kojima envisioned a boss called Decoy Octopus. The boss would blend in with its environment, causing confusion to Snake and tricking the player repeatedly. This idea was greeted with joy - what a fantastic, visionary villain! The problem was that the PlayStation 1 had no chance of coping with that sort of programming, so it was dropped and implemented in the fourth title years later as Laughing Octopus. As a boss fight, it's quite exceptional and well worth a look.

7. The unfortunate end to *Metal Gear Solid,* as the fans know it, comes with the fifth game, *The Phantom Pain*. Though a really fun game that threw the series in a different stylistic direction, it always felt unfinished. This is because it *was* unfinished. Kojima was thrown off of the project, along with his team, and he was banned from contributing to the rest of the game. As a result, the end feels rushed with many character arcs just sort of...stopping. Kojima was also banned from attending The Game Awards show in 2015, which was interested in honoring him. Many fans feel that Konami was heavy-handed and that it would have been better to resolve things amicably. (This also brought the end to the horror project *P.T.*, which had been designed by Kojima for Konami).

CONCLUSION

So, we come to the end of this little encyclopedia of gaming facts and factoids. Hopefully, you've thoroughly enjoyed yourself and laughed, even if the joke was aimed at your favorite game.

This book was a joy to construct by this little gamer nerd; with any luck, you've been able to tell that it takes one to know one.

For much of its existence, gaming has been seen as a minor art form, if an art form at all. It's been belittled as a form of entertainment, leading parents to scoff at their kid's latest obsession, while watching their sixth hour of TV that evening. Today, the new parents are gamers themselves, and remember the joy that their first console brought them. Or perhaps they recall their first visit to the online multiplayer world, where they laughed derisively as they blasted their best friend's head off with an RPG. It's all good.

The kids today are in a world that's more accepting of video games and gamers in general. Streamers will be irritating, YouTubers will overpopulate their content with adverts, and children as young as 11 will still swear at you while you play *Call of Duty*. But for many of us gamers who've been around to have seen some of the past millennium, we can tell that the younger lot inhabit a more accepting world that is better populated with quality games. Although none of them can beat *Tony Hawk's Pro Skater 2*. Sorry, that wasn't included, perhaps in the next addition.

Continue to find joy in the video games you play, read about the history of it all, and understand that just because it was 2D and pixely, it doesn't mean it wasn't magical.

Printed in Great Britain
by Amazon

48314170R00116